Essential Histories

The Soviet-Afghan War
1979–89

Essential Histories

The Soviet–Afghan War
1979–89

Gregory Fremont-Barnes

First published in Great Britain in 2012 by Osprey Publishing,
Midland House, West Way, Botley, Oxford, OX2 0PH, UK
44-02 23rd Street, Suite 219, Long Island City, NY 11101, USA

E-mail: info@ospreypublishing.com

Osprey Publishing is part of the Osprey Group

A CIP catalogue record for this book is available from the British
Library

Print ISBN: 978 1 84908 805 3
PDF ebook ISBN: 978 1 84908 854 1
ePub ebook ISBN: 978 1 78200 321 2

Page layout by The Black Spot
Index by Marie-Pierre Evans
Typeset in ITC Stone Serif and Gill Sans
Maps by Peter Bull Art Studio
Originated by PDQ Media, Bungay, UK
Printed in Hong Kong through Bookbuilders

12 13 14 15 16   10 9 8 7 6 5 4 3 2 1

Osprey Publishing is supporting the Woodland Trust, the UK's
leading woodland conservation charity, by funding the dedication
of trees.

Contents

Introduction

Its significance often overlooked, the Soviet–Afghan War stands as one of the seminal events of the last quarter of the 20th century. In less than a decade it exposed fatal defects in the Soviet political structure as well as in communist ideology itself, helped trigger and sustain the policy of internal reform led by Mikhail Gorbachev (1931–) from 1985, contributed strongly to the collapse of the communist party and the consequent end to the Cold War and, finally, played a decisive contributing role in the disintegration of the USSR. The conflict rapidly involved other nations with strong political interests at stake in Central Asia, not least the United States, which clandestinely siphoned billions of dollars in aid to the mujahideen through Pakistan. Pakistan itself not only strongly supported the resistance in general, but particularly those elements of religious extremists who in the wake of Soviet withdrawal took a prominent part in the internecine struggle between rival mujahideen factions which ultimately led to the Taliban's triumph in the autumn of 1996. In short, the network that became al-Qaeda took root as a direct consequence of the Soviet–Afghan War, in which Osama bin Laden and others like him provided substantial funds to large numbers of jihadi.

The international implications soon became apparent. Quite apart from the horrific wave of repression which their regime unleashed, the Taliban offered Afghanistan as a training and recruiting ground for other extremist groups whose political and ideological agenda stretched far beyond the borders of their war-ravaged country. By hosting al-Qaeda on Afghan soil,

Nuristani resistance fighters at prayer, January 1980. The moral inspiration of Islam proved a significant factor in the defeat of Soviet forces, whose motivation rested largely in the instinct for survival rather than in any deep-seated moral, religious or ideological conviction. (© Alain Dejean/Sygma/Corbis)

Soviet convoy in the Salang Pass, through which massive supply columns, some numbering several hundred vehicles, travelled nearly 300 miles (483km) over the Hindu Kush to Kabul. Contrary to popular belief, the Soviets did not enter Afghanistan in overwhelming force; instead, Moscow only committed troops on a limited basis. This proved a fatal error, for the sheer geographical size of Afghanistan absorbed Soviet forces like a sponge. Moreover, the Soviet military was not designed for the sort of fighting it would encounter there. Neither its doctrine or strategy nor its operational or tactical methods were intended for operations other than in central and western Europe or along the Soviet–Chinese border, against an enemy similarly armed and operating according to methods familiar to Soviet strategists and soldiers. (© Michel Setboun/Corbis)

the Taliban sowed the seeds for the terrorist attacks of 11 September 2001, which in turn triggered a devastating reaction from the United States and the United Kingdom, soon followed by other NATO powers. All of this 'Pandora's box' may be traced to the Soviet invasion of Afghanistan and the ghastly war it inaugurated.

The foundations of a full understanding of the West's involvement in Afghanistan today must rest upon a firm grasp of the causes, course and outcome of the

Soviet–Afghan War. The lessons from this confirmed the folly that underpinned Soviet strategy: unrealistic political aims, pursued by armed forces unable to cope with the unconventional methods of an adversary which, though vastly disadvantaged in weapons and technology, managed to overcome the odds through sheer tenacity and an unswerving devotion to freedom and faith.

In 1979, political leaders in Moscow directed a sceptical military to intervene in the Afghan civil war in order to maintain in power a nominally communist regime in Kabul, which was struggling against a resistance movement of disparate groups known collectively as the mujahideen or 'fighters for the faith'. Deeply unpopular with large swathes of rural, deeply conservative, tribal peoples stretched across a country divided on religious, ethnic and tribal lines, Nur Mohammed Taraki's (1913(?)–79) government of the Democratic Republic of Afghanistan (DRA) controlled urban areas but very little of the countryside, where tribal elders and clan chiefs held sway. Even within the communist party apparatus, rival factions grappled for sole control of the affairs of state, denying them the time or ability to implement the socialist reforms they espoused, including the emancipation of women, land redistribution and the dismantling of traditional societal structures in favour of a more egalitarian alternative. None of these reforms resonated with a traditional, Islamic nation, whose opposition manifested its outrage in open civil war. Taraki was overthrown by his own prime minister – a member of the opposing communist faction – but he proved even less effective at imposing rule than his predecessor. Lack of political direction and anger at unwanted reforms precipitated mutinies and mass desertions within the army and outbreaks of bloody revolt in cities, towns and villages across the country, which the Soviets immediately appreciated as a threat to their influence over a neighbouring state sharing a border with three of the USSR's Muslim republics.

Leonid Brezhnev (1906–82), the General Secretary of the Communist Party of the Soviet Union, concerned at the disintegrating situation in Afghanistan and determined to maintain a sphere of influence over the region, ordered an invasion – despite the fact that neither the climate nor the terrain suited Soviet equipment or tactics. When Soviet troops rolled over the border in December 1979, ostensibly in aid of a surrogate government in Kabul, they expected to conduct a brief, largely bloodless campaign with highly sophisticated mechanized and air assault forces, easily capable of crushing Afghan resistance in a matter of months before enabling a newly installed government to tackle the resistance thereafter. Events exploded at least two myths prevalent in the West: the Soviets never intended to remain long in Afghanistan, as supposed in Washington, and their relatively small troop numbers attested to this fact. Nor did the invasion represent the belated realization of the historic Russian drive to establish a warm-water port on the Indian Ocean. Theirs was to be a temporary – albeit an internationally condemned – presence.

Yet the Soviets comprehensively failed to appreciate the quagmire in which they found themselves. Their forces possessed very limited combat experience – none at all in counterinsurgency – and they foolishly assumed their successful interventions in East Germany in 1954, in Hungary in 1956 and in Czechoslovakia in 1968 offered models for any military operation executed against a popular struggle. Western analysts, too, predicted Soviet victory, but the political and military circumstances behind the Iron Curtain offered no parallels with Afghanistan. Unlike the Soviets' client states in Eastern Europe, Afghanistan stood embroiled in the midst of a civil war – not a straightforward, effectively unarmed, insurrection – and thus applying simple but overwhelming military might could only guarantee protection for the central government in Kabul, and perhaps control of larger cities and towns, but not the countryside. Soviet intervention in December 1979 achieved its initial objective with predictable ease: elite troops overthrew the government, seized the presidential palace and key communications centres, killed the head of state, Hafizullah Amin (1929–79), and replaced him with a Soviet-sponsored successor.

The plan thereafter seemed straightforward: stabilize the political situation, strengthen, re-train and enlarge DRA forces to enable them to quell the insurgency on their own while concurrently performing the more passive roles of garrison duty and, finally, protect the country's key infrastructure such as major roads, dams and its sources of electricity and gas. Thus, within three years, the Soviets, confident in the notion that the Afghan government could stand on its own feet when backed by the continued presence of Soviet advisors including army officers, KGB personnel, civilian specialists in engineering, medicine, education and other spheres, and furnished with a continuous supply of arms and technology, believed their forces could withdraw across the border, leaving a friendly, stable, compliant and ideologically like-minded regime firmly in power behind them.

None of these objectives stood up to the reality of the situation, however. The civil war continued to spiral beyond the government's ability to suppress it and the DRA forces' morale plummeted further, decreasing their operational effectiveness and causing concern in Moscow that withdrawing its troops would amount to both humiliation and the collapse of all Soviet influence over its client state. Thus, what began as a fairly simple military operation – overthrowing a government and occupying key positions throughout the country, a task which the Soviet military,

Ahmed Shah Massoud (with walking stick) relaxing amongst some of his fighters in the Panjshir Valley, June 1985. On the face of it, the mujahideen stood little chance of defeating so formidable a force as the Soviet 40th Army, for the resistance lacked high technology or heavy weapons, possessed limited supplies of what armaments they did have, and boasted no formal organization, co-ordinated strategy or unified effort. Still, sheer determination heavily compensated for some of their deficiencies. (© Reza/Webistan/Corbis)

practised by opponents trained and armed to fight in central Europe – against troops of utterly different organization and doctrine. Experience soon demonstrated the limited efficacy of heavy infantry, tanks, artillery, and jet fighters in a struggle that decisively depended upon more helicopter gunships, more heliborne troops, and more special forces to meet the demands of the fluid, asymmetric war conducted by the mujahideen.

As the years passed and casualties steadily mounted, the war graphically exposed the weaknesses of the Soviets' strategy and the poorly suited structure of their armed forces, which never succeeded in overcoming an ever-growing resistance movement operating over a vast, varied and exceedingly challenging landscape. Indeed, both Soviet tactics and strategy contained fatal flaws. Their doctrine directed the use of armoured and motor-rifle (i.e motorized) units to advance along narrow axes, maintaining secure lines of communication while wreaking destruction upon any resistance they encountered through combined arms (the co-ordination of firepower offered by infantry, artillery, armour and air assault units). With little experience or training in a counterinsurgency role, the Soviet armed forces chose a simplistic approach to the problem: they merely cleared territory in their path, which translated into the widespread killing of civilians, as well as resistance fighters – who avoided where possible the superior weight of fire which their opponents could bring to bear. Everywhere circumstances appeared to confirm Alexander the Great's dictum

trained in large-scale, high-tempo operations could manage with ease – soon developed into a protracted, costly and ultimately unwinnable fiasco. The conflict pitted small, ill-armed but highly motivated guerrilla forces – employing fighting methods bearing no relation to those that 'one can occupy Afghanistan, but one cannot vanquish her'.

Civilians who survived the onslaught naturally fled, embittered, abandoning their destroyed villages and property to seek refuge in cities or over the border. Such ruthless exploitation of air and artillery power was deliberately meant to clear areas, particularly along the border with Pakistan, so as to deprive the resistance of recruits and local support as well as to aid in the interdiction of supplies crossing over into Afghanistan. This strategy caused horrendous human suffering: only six months after the Soviet invasion, approximately 800,000 Afghans had fled into Pakistan.

At the outset of the war the Soviets' strategy involved persuading the population to support the communist-led Kabul government, thus denying aid to the resistance in the anonymity of the provinces. This soon proved unrealistic, not least owing to the regime's heavy-handed measures. They then turned to denying the insurgents supplies, which led to driving civilians off their land or destroying their livelihoods as a warning to withhold their support from the insurgency. This policy also involved interdicting supply routes that connected the insurgents to the vital matériel moving through Pakistan, the principal source of aid to the mujahideen. The Soviet 40th Army mounted numerous substantial operations against areas known to be actively supporting the resistance and severed supply lines whenever possible, but the 'drip, drip' effect caused by the guerrillas' constant ambushes, sniping, raids and mine-laying ultimately inflicted unsustainable losses on the invader.

The Soviet–Afghan War differed from other conflicts of the Cold War era. Although it was a limited conflict, it was longer than most – slightly over nine years in length –

and thus did not share the decisive nature of the Arab–Israeli wars of 1948, 1956, 1967 and 1973, or the Falklands War of 1982. The Soviet *imbroglio* lacked the scale of either the Korean War (1950–53) or Vietnam (1965–73) and did not conclude with a clear political outcome, in contrast to those proxy conflicts. Nor can it be seen as some sort of Soviet 'Vietnam', especially in terms of scale. The Soviets never deployed anything approaching the numbers the Americans sent to Southeast Asia, with over half a million personnel by 1968, compared with the average of approximately 118,000 Soviets serving at any given time in Afghanistan. Whereas the Americans conducted numerous operations involving several divisions, the Soviets' entire 40th Army in Afghanistan consisted of a mere five divisions, four independent brigades and four independent regiments, plus various small support units. Numbers as insufficient as these denied the Soviets – by their own faulty strategic calculations – any realistic chance of securing over 20 provincial centres plus various key industrial sites, to say nothing of the manpower required to secure whole swathes of remote and practically inaccessible territory inhabited by a seething population supporting elusive, seldom-visible opponents who moved by stealth, struck at will, and melted back into civilian life with little or no trace. The protection demanded for hundreds of miles of roads, communication lines, and points of strategic importance – some of which the Soviets had to occupy outright or, at the very least, deny to the mujahideen – placed a colossal burden on the invaders, who failed to appreciate both the sheer scale of the enterprise and the immense commitment in manpower it required.

Chronology

1965 **1 January** People's Democratic Party
of Afghanistan (PDPA) is founded,
giving the communists a stake
in Afghan politics.

1973 **July** Mohammed Daoud Khan
(1909–78) ends the 40-year reign
of King Mohammed Zahir Shah
(1915–2007) in a palace coup.

1978 **17 April** President Daoud is
assassinated in a communist coup
led by Nur Mohammed Taraki, who
appoints himself head of state and
begins a reign of terror against
political opponents.

1979 **15–21 March** Anti-communist
demonstrators take control of Herat;
the Afghan 15th Division, ordered
to retake the city, deserts to the
resistance. Afghan and Soviet air
forces bomb the city, killing an
estimated 5,000 civilians.
17 March Soviet Politburo debates
question of internal situation
in Afghanistan.
20 March Despite Taraki's urgent
request for Soviet intervention in
the Afghan civil war, Soviet Foreign
Minister Alexei Kosygin (1904–80)
declines, fearing escalation of violence.
April Helicopters manned by Soviet
pilots in support of a DRA offensive
in the Kunar Valley destroy the
village of Kerala in Kunar province,
killing approximately 1,000 people.
17 May Mechanized brigade of
the Afghan 7th Division defects to
the mujahideen in Paktia province.
August 5th Brigade of the Afghan
9th Division mutinies and supports
the rebels in the Kunar Valley.

14 September Troops loyal to
Prime Minister Hafizullah Amin kill
Taraki, enabling Amin to take power.
4 November Iranian militants
storm the US Embassy in Tehran,
inadvertently diverting the attention
of the Carter administration from
deteriorating events in Afghanistan.
12 December Soviet Politburo reaches
decision for invasion
of Afghanistan.
24 December Soviet air assault
forces arrive in Kabul by air.
27 December Large-scale Soviet
forces cross into Afghanistan by
road and proceed south; Soviet air
assault and Spetsnaz forces stage
a coup in Kabul and kill Amin.
28 December Babrak Karmal
(1929–96) appointed new head
of state of the Democratic Republic
of Afghanistan.

1980 **1 January** Revolt in Kandahar results
in deaths of Soviet troops and citizens
by mob violence.
January United Nations condemns
the Soviet invasion.
February Soviet forces conduct
sweep of Kunar Valley.
21 February Soviet Army and
KGB forces kill hundreds and arrest
thousands (many later executed) of
Afghans protesting the occupation of
their country; massive demonstrations
in Kabul; anti-Soviet riot suppressed
by Soviet forces in Shindand,
in Farah province.
March Soviet offensive in Paktia
province; second sweep of Kunar
Valley.
April Soviet offensive in Panjshir
Valley.

Afghanistan (physical and political)

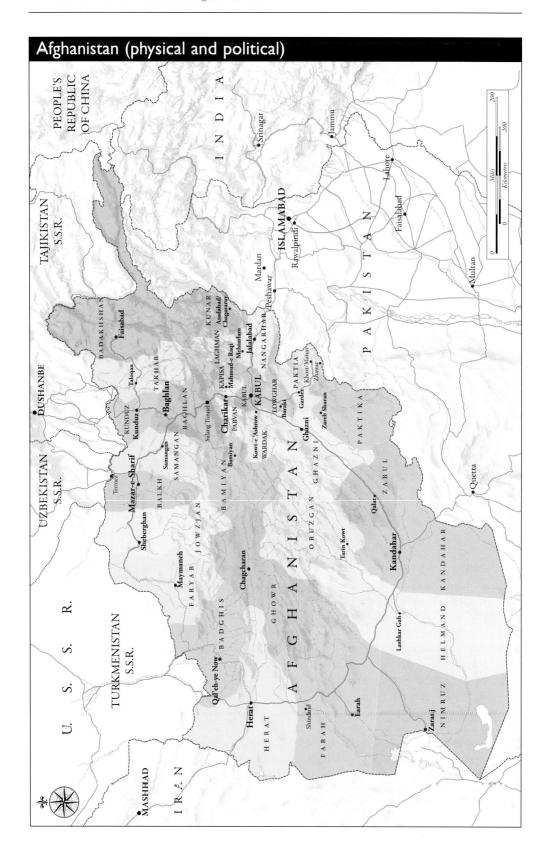

May Soviet forces sweep Ghazni province; third sweep of Kunar Valley.
June Second sweep of Ghazni province.
September Fourth sweep of Kunar Valley; *Panjshir I* operation.
October *Panjshir II* offensive.
November Fifth sweep of Kunar Valley; sweep of Wardak province; Soviet offensive in Lowghar Valley until mid-December.

Mujahideen in the Panjshir Valley, June 1985. Contrary to popular belief, the mujahideen did not enjoy universal support in the villages, where some inhabitants requested their departure lest their presence invite air attack. Sometimes the resistance took food and yet offered no help in repairing bomb damage, developing schools, or administering political or social programmes on the model of Mao, Ho Chi Minh or Fidel Castro. (© Reza/Webistan/Corbis)

December Sweep in Nangarhar province; fighting in Herat.

1981 20 January Ronald Reagan (1911–2004) succeeds Jimmy Carter (1924–) as US President.
February–March Fighting in Kandahar.
April *Panjshir III* offensive.
June–July Soviet offensive in Nangarhar province.
4 July Offensive in Sarobi Valley in Paktika province; fighting in Herat.
August *Panjshir IV* offensive.
5 September Offensive in Farah province.
October Soviet sweep around Herat; offensive in Kandahar.

1982 January Fighting in Herat.
1 January Javier Pérez de Cuéllar (1920–) succeeds Kurt Waldheim (1918–2007) as UN Secretary General.
February Urban fighting in Kandahar.
May *Panjshir V* offensive, launched in retaliation for mujahideen attack on Bagram air base.
July Sweep of Paghman Hills west of Kabul.
August–September *Panjshir VI* offensive.
November Offensive in Laghman Valley.

10 November Brezhnev dies; succeeded by Yuri Andropov (1914–84) as General Secretary of the Communist Party of the Soviet Union.

1983 **January** Offensive in Lowghar Valley.
February UN Secretary General Pérez de Cuéllar discusses Soviet withdrawal with Andropov.
April Sweep around Herat.
June Offensive in Ghazni province.
August Offensive in Paktia province.
November Offensive in Shomali Valley.

1984 **9 February** Andropov dies; succeeded by Konstantin Chernenko (1911–85) as General Secretary of the Communist Party of the Soviet Union.
April *Panjshir VII* offensive.
June Offensive in the Lowghar Valley; offensives around Herat and Kandahar.
July–August Offensive in Lowghar and Shomali valleys.
August–October Soviet forces relieve garrison of Ali Kheyl in Paktia province.
September *Panjshir VIII* offensive.
October Fighting in Herat.
November Operation in Paktia province.
December Offensive in Kunar Valley.

1985 **10 March** Chernenko dies; succeeded by Mikhail Gorbachev.
April Offensive in the Maidan Valley in Wardak province.
May–June Offensive in Kunar province and relief of the garrison at Barikowt.
June *Panjshir IX* offensive.
July Fighting in Herat and Kandahar.
August–September Offensive in Paktia province; Khost is relieved but Soviet forces fail to capture Zhawar.
October Soviet Politburo decides troops should leave Afghanistan within 18 months.

1986 **February** Gorbachev announces to 27th Soviet Party Congress that troops will leave Afghanistan.
March Offensive around Andkhvoy.
April Zhawar captured during offensive in Paktia province.
May Offensive near Kandahar.
5 May Mohammad Najibullah Ahmadzai (1947–96) replaces Karmal as People's Democratic Party of Afghanistan (PDPA) General Secretary and effective head of state.
c. June–August Soviets withdraw 15,000 troops from Afghanistan.
June Offensive in Khejob Valley.
August Offensive in Lowghar Valley.
September First Stinger missiles deployed in action by mujahideen, bringing down three helicopters.
October Withdrawal of six Soviet regiments.
November Offensive in Mizan Valley in Oruzgan province.

1987 **May–June** Offensive in Paktia province.
November Start of Soviets' Operation *Magistral* to relieve Khost.
December Khost relieved; Gorbachev and Reagan discuss Afghanistan at the Washington Summit.

1988 **March** Offensive in Paktika province to relieve Orgun.
April Offensive between Kandahar and Ghazni.
14 April Conclusion of Geneva Accords, which had begun informally three years before; agreements for Soviet withdrawal.
May–August Large-scale withdrawals by 40th Army from various points in Afghanistan.
15 October Strength of Soviet forces in Afghanistan down to half to approximately 60,000.
November Start of second phase of large-scale withdrawals by 40th Army from various points in Afghanistan, but mainly the south.

1989   **20 January** George H. W. Bush (1924–) succeeds Ronald Reagan as US President.
15 February Withdrawal of the last Soviet combat units from Afghanistan.

1992   **15–16 April** Najibullah's regime collapses.
August Russian Embassy in Kabul evacuated.

1996   **September** Taliban forces capture Kabul and execute Najibullah.

2001   **11 September** al-Qaeda launches terrorist attacks against the United States, killing 3,000 people in the Twin Towers in New York and others at the Pentagon in Washington and aboard an airliner which crashes in the Pennsylvania countryside.
December US and UK forces, together with those of the Afghan Northern Alliance, oust the Taliban from government; thereafter, other NATO forces arrive to oppose continued Taliban resistance and to drive al-Qaeda from the country.

Afghans in Kacha Garhi refugee camp in Pakistan, March 1983. The policy of driving vast numbers of rural dwellers off the land typified the Soviets' ruthless and short-sighted approach to counterinsurgency, for their near-total failure to implement a 'hearts and minds' campaign stirred the wrath of untold numbers of men and boys who joined the ranks of the mujahideen both to recover their independence and to escape the squalid conditions of the refugee camps. (© Alain Keler/Sygma/Corbis)

The genesis of Afghan–Russian relations

The roots of Russian intervention in Afghanistan extend back to imperial times, when Tsarist Russia first cast its eyes on Central Asia in the 1730s. Russia undertook the gradual conquest of the region as part of an expansionist programme, which witnessed Russian growth into the Crimea, the Caucasus, and Siberia all the way to the Pacific. By the late 1830s Russian interest in Afghanistan in particular began to manifest itself. Following the Russo-Persian War of 1826–28, the Russians began to exercise modest influence within government circles in Tehran, and when in 1837 Persian forces sought to capture Herat, in western Afghanistan, Russian advisors and mercenaries accompanied the expedition. Authorities in Calcutta – the capital of British India and the seat of the East India Company, which managed Britain's Indian dominions – concerned at the growing Russian menace to Afghan independence, threatened intervention and managed to instigate a Persian withdrawal, but from this point Anglo-Russian relations began to sour. Herein lay the beginnings of the 'Great Game' – a contest for influence in Central Asia, but specifically over Afghanistan and the unclear border regions on the northern fringes of the Raj. As Russian power expanded inexorably into the Caucasus, Georgia and Khirgiz, and towards the khanates of Samarkand, Khiva and Bukhara, the British foresaw the point when their position in India would lie exposed to Russia – once the buffer of Afghanistan fell under the Romanovs' sway. Nor was it inconceivable that the Russians ultimately sought access to a warm-water port by occupying Afghanistan before penetrating south, across what now constitutes Pakistan, to the coast of the Indian Ocean.

British suspicions of Russian intentions took a dramatic turn when British and East India Company forces invaded Afghanistan in 1839 in order to counter perceived Russian influence at the Afghan court. In fact, the Afghans had declined to receive the Russian diplomatic representative at Kabul even before the Anglo-Indian army crossed the frontier, rendering the entire exercise costly and pointless, and bruising Britain's martial reputation after a three-year occupation of Afghanistan. Nevertheless, suspicions of Russian intentions continued thereafter, despite the drubbing inflicted on the tsar by the British and French during the Crimean War (1854–56), which thwarted imperial expansion against Turkey and into the Mediterranean. The war checked Russia's expansion into the Danubian provinces (modern Romania and Bulgaria) and towards the Bosphorus and Dardanelles (the Black Sea straits), but she merely re-directed her energies against Central Asia, so that by 1869 the Russian frontier reached the Amu Darya River (the classical Oxus) on the northern border of Afghanistan, to much alarm in London and Calcutta. The next crisis occurred in 1878, when, in the midst of another war with Turkey in which Russia sought to control the Black Sea straits, St Petersburg again dispatched a diplomatic mission to Kabul, provoking a second British invasion of Afghanistan. After achieving a rather better military and political outcome than their previous campaign almost 40 years before, the British withdrew in 1881, content with having extracted various concessions, including the right to regulate Afghan foreign policy thereafter. The 'Great Game' cannot be said to have come to an end until 1907 when, with the Anglo-Russian treaty of that year – fresh on the heels of the Russians' decisive defeat at the hands of the Japanese in Manchuria in 1904–05 – St Petersburg declared that Afghanistan stood outside her sphere of influence and promised to consult Britain on all business concerning Russia and Afghanistan. In a *quid pro quo*, Britain pledged neither to occupy nor to annex any Afghan territory nor to meddle in its domestic affairs. Afghanistan did not recognize this agreement, but the terms remained in force between the imperial powers until 1919, when Afghan troops crossed into India and tried to foment an insurrection along the frontier – a matter settled in the very brief Third Anglo-Afghan War (May–August 1919) in which Britain ejected the invaders before agreeing to forswear all control over Afghan foreign policy and thus signifying the country's status as a genuinely sovereign state.

The war offered the Afghans the opportunity to request military aid from the new Bolshevik government and, while the conflict ended before anything materialized, the episode inaugurated a close relationship between Afghanistan and the Soviet Union. This resulted in the 1921 Afghan–Soviet Treaty, the first international agreement concluded by the new Soviet state, marking the beginning of economic and military aid to Kabul. Thereafter, the Soviets intervened on two occasions: once in 1925 to occupy a small disputed island in the Amu Darya, and four years later, after the overthrow of King Amanullah (1892–1960; reigned 1919–29), when a Soviet force intervened in a failed attempt to return him to office. International calls for the troops' withdrawal forced the issue, but in 1930 Soviet troops again crossed the frontier in pursuit of a dissident who sought protection in neutral Afghanistan.

During the 1920s and '30s, the Soviets concentrated on suppressing (successfully) various guerrilla movements that sprang up after the Central Asian territories refused to accept control from Moscow. With British withdrawal from India in 1947 (which led to partition, with Pakistan emerging as Afghanistan's eastern and southern neighbour), the Soviets no longer faced any serious competitor in the region for influence

Entrance to the Bolan Pass in Baluchistan during the First Anglo-Afghan War (1839–42), after a watercolour by James Atkinson. British suspicions of Russian intentions in Afghanistan led to an invasion by Anglo-Indian troops, who sought to replace the regime with one disposed to keeping Russian influence at bay and encouraging strong ties with the Governor-General of (British) India. (© Stapleton Collection/Corbis)

over Afghanistan, and their interest in the area redoubled, particularly after Stalin's death in 1953, when Soviet arms poured into the country as part of a larger financial-aid package and a drive towards increased levels of trade. In January 1954, for example, Prime Minister Daoud secured a Soviet loan of $3.5 million to aid in the construction of two silos and bakeries, while the following year the two countries renewed a barter protocol on commodity exchange that guaranteed Soviet imports, including petroleum, construction materials (especially cement) and metals, in exchange for Afghan wool, raw cotton and animal hides. In December 1955, the Soviet Union granted a $100 million, long-term development loan for the purpose of undertaking projects jointly agreed by surveyors from both countries. This massive

Pedestrian traffic in Kabul, January 1980. By devastating large agricultural areas during the war, the Soviets drove much of the population off the land and into the cities, where the authorities artificially lowered prices to attract the displaced to areas that troops could easily control. The policy became so widespread that many rural-dwellers paradoxically came to depend on sources of food from urban areas. (© Bettmann/Corbis)

influx of Soviet investment funded the building of roads, river ports, an improved telecommunications network, hydroelectric plants, irrigation dams with canal systems, bridges, hospitals, hydroelectric dams, airfields and the Salang Pass highway tunnel, which provided a route through the practically impenetrable Hindu Kush mountain range from the north. Simultaneously, Daoud secured a ten-year extension of the 1931 Soviet–Afghan Treaty of Neutrality and Non-Aggression. In March 1956, on the strength of recommendations made by Soviet advisors, the Afghans launched the first Five Year Plan, a direct parallel to that initiated under Stalin in the 1930s.

Officially, Afghanistan remained a neutral, non-aligned nation, staying aloof from Cold War politics, but in reality, it was moving inexorably into the Soviet sphere, not through ideological inclination, but by dint of growing economic dependence. Naturally, the further Soviet–Afghan relations deepened, the stronger Moscow's inclination was to protect its investment by carefully cultivating its neighbour. As with so many other developing nations, the Soviets exploited Afghanistan as a testing ground for the peaceful economic penetration of a 'Third World' nation as part of their world-wide programme of competition with capitalist states. By the early 1960s, many Eastern Bloc products found markets in Afghanistan, especially goods from Czechoslovakia and Poland, both of which provided loans and barter agreements.

As the Americans refused Kabul military assistance, the Afghans naturally turned to the Soviets, who in August 1956 concluded an agreement to supply $25 million in arms, including tanks, bombers, helicopters and small arms, as well as to provide expertise in

constructing or expanding military airfields. The Afghans' dependence on spare parts and technical assistance in turn drew in Soviet military advisors, who served in large numbers attached to Afghan military units and their training establishments, while 4,000 Afghan officers received education and training in the Soviet Union, prompting many, indoctrinated with Marxist principles, to establish a communist party at home on 1 January 1965. By the 1970s the Soviets had established a strong influence over Afghan

affairs, a circumstance that enabled a small group of communist-inspired Afghan army officers to seize control of the government and establish the Democratic Republic of Afghanistan (DRA) in 1978 under Nur Mohammed Taraki.

The Soviets harboured a strong desire not to forfeit the colossal financial investment made in Afghanistan over more than two decades, and sought to bolster the tenuously established communist regime on its border, which justified their support on ideological grounds. Above all, Moscow hoped to prevent an Islamic government – whether as radical as that ensconced in Tehran in February 1979 or not – from overthrowing Taraki's government. Any such successor government, motivated by militant Islam, would pose a threat to the stability of the Soviet Union's Central Asian republics of Tajikistan, Turkmenistan and Uzbekistan, which between them accounted for 60 million Muslims spread right across the vulnerable southern flank of the Soviet empire.

Moscow and the mujahideen

Soviet forces and their DRA allies

The 40th Army, which represented the Soviets' military presence in Afghanistan, varied in strength, but averaged around 118,000 men in Afghanistan at any given time. These troops were never intended to play the leading role in subduing the Afghan insurgency – that was to remain the primary responsibility of DRA forces – and never anticipated the scale of the enterprise triggered by their appearance on Afghan soil. As a consequence, and because of the Kremlin's steadfast adherence to the original notion that the 40th Army remain a 'limited contingent', these troops failed to establish the substantial presence in the country that subsequent events rendered so necessary. Moreover, with their armed forces structured, equipped and trained to operate on the northern European plain (or Central Front, in NATO parlance), or alternatively on the plains of northern China as the most likely battlegrounds of the future, Soviet strategists expected to conduct fast-paced conventional operations. They certainly did not anticipate undertaking a low-intensity, asymmetric war in Central Asia, and thus their force structure, weaponry and tactics necessarily underwent substantial alteration, a programme which of course took time to evolve and implement.

Broadly speaking, Soviet troops engaged in four types of military action in Afghanistan. The first consisted of major operations conducted by both regular and special forces, including artillery and aircraft, and generally in conjunction with DRA units, the purpose being to destroy large groups of mujahideen in particular areas of the country. Soviet commanders conducted these operations in phases lasting for several weeks or longer.

Young Soviet air assault paratrooper. Equipment and gear better suited to Afghan conditions was supplied to mountain rifle battalions and to Spetsnaz, but was never available in sufficient quantities for general issue across the army. The troops needed modern, load-bearing packs, less restrictive clothing, lightweight, warm and waterproof sleeping bags (as opposed to those supplied to them which readily absorbed water and gained several pounds in weight), as well as boots designed for the excessive wear-and-tear of operations over rough, often mountainous, terrain. (© Patrick Robert/Sygma/Corbis)

The second type of operation was carried out on a smaller scale, perhaps by a single regiment with artillery and aircraft in support. This type of operation focused on destroying a specific group of rebels in a location discovered via intelligence gathering. Such operations tended to be conducted in ten days or less. Thirdly, while such combat missions were under way, units 'combed' villages in search of concealed weapons caches or medical aid stations. Fourthly, small units, often company-sized, conducted ambushes along roads, on mountain trails and near villages, with locations selected on the basis of intelligence gathered by Afghan intelligence personnel.

Even so, to a considerable extent the Soviets remained shackled to the methods they knew and understood – large-scale operations in the form of conventional offensives. They continued to launch these regularly, most notably in the Panjshir Valley, despite generally poor results, since none of these major operations achieved more than temporarily neutralizing resistance activity in the areas over which the Soviets' ponderous military machine functioned. Experience revealed that heliborne forces operating in conjunction with mechanized forces could function effectively at the battalion and brigade level, but such methods tended to stifle tactical success when carried out on a divisional or larger scale. Counterinsurgency depends on highly mobile, well-led, well-trained and suitably equipped forces capable of fighting guerrillas by employing their own methods. Soviet armour, airpower and heavily laden infantry dependent on their armoured personnel carriers (APCs) for transport over difficult terrain could not, despite their impressive firepower, compensate for their inherent shortcomings in a counterinsurgency environment, for the mujahideen seldom appeared in concentration, and in any event disappeared before Soviet troops could bring that overwhelming firepower to bear.

The terrain of Afghanistan is heavily mountainous, although the country consists of extensive areas of dry plains, deserts and 'green zones' of river valleys and vegetation as well. This mountainous terrain strongly influenced the strategy adopted by the Soviets, obliging their commanders to convey troops to an operational area via helicopter or convoy. Whenever possible, they sent troops ahead of the main body or inserted advance parties of troops by helicopter on to high ground to cover

those following behind. Yet this of course depended on the availability of such aircraft, required proper planning and exposed the limited number of helicopters to ground fire, especially rocket-propelled grenades (RPGs) and Stingers (hand-held, ground-to-air rocket launchers).

Close to the larger cities and along frequently travelled roads the Soviets established permanent posts consisting of garrisons of between 15 and 40 troops, who controlled the immediate area, guarded the roads and guided artillery fire. Owing to their isolation, they could call on help via

Soviet soldier in winter gear. The Soviets frequently sought to destroy mujahideen forces through envelopment, whereby forces of company or battalion strength were detached from the main body and sent to threaten the enemy flank or rear in support of the advance of the main body. Similarly, such detachments might operate independently and launch a simultaneous attack, preferably by surprise, from a different direction or block the retreat of mujahideen as the might of the main body began to bear down on them. (© Patrick Robert/Sygma/Corbis)

The Mi-24 Hind helicopter gunship was introduced during the war and performed well, but while the Soviets altered and improved air assault and helicopter gunship tactics throughout the course of the war, they could never deploy sufficient numbers of either type of asset to meet their needs, despite approximately 350 operational in Afghanistan and perhaps half as many based in the Soviet Union. Thus, while all convey escorts ought to have enjoyed helicopter support, this could not be guaranteed. (MSgt Steven Turner/USAF)

radio. Some of the most successful Soviet operations involved combined operations, including air assault forces in support of a mechanized ground attack. Helicopters bearing small contingents of these troops would insert them deep in the rear and on the flanks of resistance strongholds to pin insurgents, prevent their withdrawal, destroy their bases and threaten or cut off their lines of communication. Ground troops would then advance to join up with these heliborne forces and engage trapped mujahideen, destroying them with superior firepower. Heliborne forces performed best when inserted behind rebel lines within

the range of supporting artillery, unless of course their own guns accompanied them. Operations undertaken without artillery support often ended in high casualties for the Soviets.

As guerrillas received and employed new weaponry and developed new tactics, they obliged the Soviets to adapt in turn. For a large conventional force already trying to cope with shifting political circumstances in the country, this pressure proved an unwelcome addition to their existing woes, demanding new approaches to seemingly intractable problems in the field. This meant not simply the modification of tactics, but variations to uniforms, weapons and equipment to suit changing requirements.

The 40th Army comprised a professional cadre of officers and other ranks, but conscripts and reservists formed the bulk of the formation. Like so many American draftees destined for service in Vietnam in the 1960s, they were frequently reluctant or downright unwilling to serve in a war whose purpose they did not understand and in a country about which they knew nothing. 'We were drafted at age eighteen,' the disillusioned Vladislav Tamarov recalled:

We had no choice. If you weren't in college, if you weren't disabled, if your parents didn't have a lot of money – then you were required to serve. Some young men broke their legs, some paid money [for exemption from service] … (Tamarov 2005: 16)

Those with time on their hands, such as the thousands of soldiers based in rear areas involved in maintenance, logistics or communications, could easily fall prey to narcotics addiction – heroin of course being readily available in a country where poppies flourished – with predictable effects on morale, though to be fair homesickness and boredom afflicted rear units more than drug-taking.

Naturally the Soviets possessed elite forces, too, but never in adequate numbers. While ground reconnaissance troops tended to be better trained and of a higher quality than the typical conscript belonging to a motorized rifle unit, the critical shortage of high-quality infantry often led the Soviets to employ reconnaissance personnel in combat rather than in their proper reconnaissance roles. This in turn detracted from the duty of intelligence-gathering on the ground, in compensation for which commanders foolishly relied too heavily on intelligence acquired though aerial reconnaissance, radio intercept and what little access they had to agents in the field. These sources did not always yield much of tactical use, and by assigning reconnaissance units to combat duties the Soviets neglected to make best use of their skills and consequently frequently failed to locate mujahideen forces. The most famous elite forces were the Spetsnaz or 'forces of special designation', highly trained and used in long-range reconnaissance, commando and special forces functions such as night-time ambushes. They would be helicoptered in and then proceed on foot to the ambush point, there to lie in wait for their unsuspecting quarry.

A DRA soldier, whose braid suggests he belongs to a unit guarding an important government facility. Often press-ganged into the military, these troops' term of service stood at three years until March 1984, when another year's extension led to mutinies. Moscow deemed regime troops so unreliable that the Soviets deliberately kept units under-strength lest they rise against the occupying forces. The whole force averaged about 35,000 men by 1986, but desertion, demobilization and casualties amounted to losses of 10,000 annually. (© Patrick Robert/Sygma/Corbis)

Most of the infantry carried the 7.62mm AKM assault rifle, while air assault forces carried the 5.45mm AKS-74, the latter creating more substantial injury. Soviet heavy weapons included two kinds of rocket launchers: the BM-21 *Grad* ('Hail') and the BM-27 *Uragan* ('Hurricane'). Smaller weapons included the 12.7mm DShK – a heavy machine gun – as well as PTRC guided missile launchers, unguided NURS missiles, SHMELs (portable, single-shot rocket launchers like RPGs) and mortars. The Soviets deployed various types of aircraft,

Soviet/DRA forces and mujahideen strongholds, 1980s

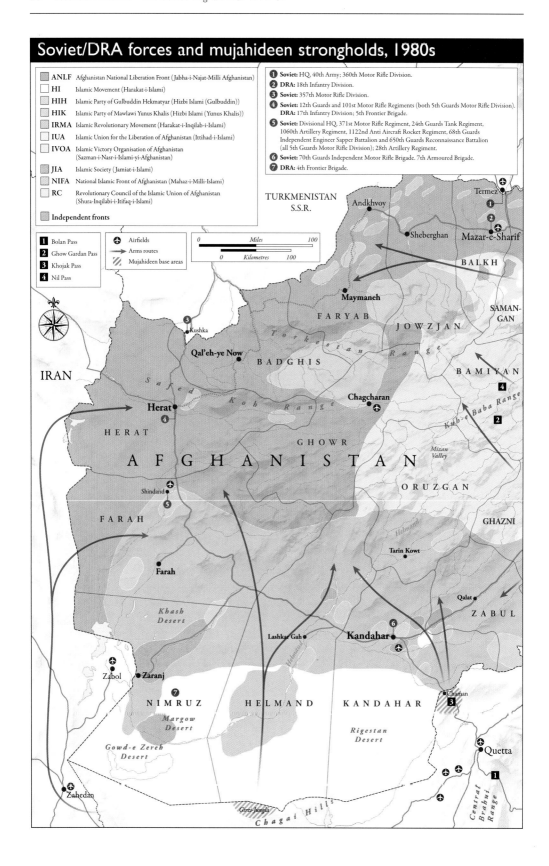

ANLF Afghanistan National Liberation Front (Jabha-i-Najat-Milli Afghanistan)
HI Islamic Movement (Harakat-i-Islami)
HIH Islamic Party of Gulbuddin Hekmatyar (Hizbi Islami (Gulbuddin))
HIK Islamic Party of Mawlawi Yunus Khalis (Hizbi Islami (Yunus Khalis))
IRMA Islamic Revolutionary Movement (Harakat-i-Inqilab-i-Islami)
IUA Islamic Union for the Liberation of Afghanistan (Ittihad-i-Islami)
IVOA Islamic Victory Organisation of Afghanistan (Sazman-i-Nasr-i-Islami-yi-Afghanistan)
JIA Islamic Society (Jamiat-i-Islami)
NIFA National Islamic Front of Afghanistan (Mahaz-i-Milli-Islami)
RC Revolutionary Council of the Islamic Union of Afghanistan (Shura-Inqilabi-Itifaq-i-Islami)

Independent fronts

① **Soviet:** HQ, 40th Army; 360th Motor Rifle Division.
② **DRA:** 18th Infantry Division.
③ **Soviet:** 357th Motor Rifle Division.
④ **Soviet:** 12th Guards and 101st Motor Rifle Regiments (both 5th Guards Motor Rifle Division). **DRA:** 17th Infantry Division; 5th Frontier Brigade.
⑤ **Soviet:** Divisional HQ, 371st Motor Rifle Regiment, 24th Guards Tank Regiment, 1060th Artillery Regiment, 1122nd Anti Aircraft Rocket Regiment, 68th Guards Independent Engineer Sapper Battalion and 650th Guards Reconnaissance Battalion (all 5th Guards Motor Rifle Division); 28th Artillery Regiment.
⑥ **Soviet:** 70th Guards Independent Motor Rifle Brigade. 7th Armoured Brigade.
⑦ **DRA:** 4th Frontier Brigade.

1 Bolan Pass
2 Ghow Gardan Pass
3 Khojak Pass
4 Nil Pass

✈ Airfields
➡ Arms routes
▨ Mujahideen base areas

Miles   0 — 100
Kilometres   0 — 100

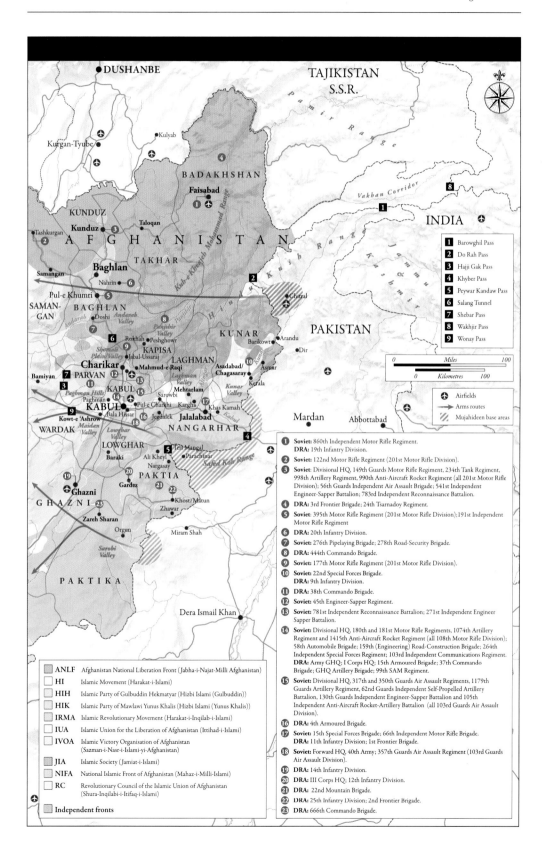

1	Barowghil Pass
2	Do Rah Pass
3	Hajji Gak Pass
4	Khyber Pass
5	Peywar Kandaw Pass
6	Salang Tunnel
7	Shebar Pass
8	Wakhjir Pass
9	Wonay Pass

Airfields
Arms routes
Mujahideen base areas

① **Soviet:** 860th Independent Motor Rifle Regiment.
DRA: 19th Infantry Division.

② **Soviet:** 122nd Motor Rifle Regiment (201st Motor Rifle Division).

③ **Soviet:** Divisional HQ, 149th Guards Motor Rifle Regiment, 234th Tank Regiment, 998th Artillery Regiment, 990th Anti-Aircraft Rocket Regiment (all 201st Motor Rifle Division); 56th Guards Independent Air Assault Brigade; 541st Independent Engineer-Sapper Battalion; 783rd Independent Reconnaissance Battalion.
DRA: 3rd Frontier Brigade; 24th Tsarnadoy Regiment.

④ **DRA:** 3rd Frontier Brigade; 24th Tsarnadoy Regiment.

⑤ **Soviet:** 395th Motor Rifle Regiment (201st Motor Rifle Division);191st Independent Motor Rifle Regiment

⑥ **DRA:** 20th Infantry Division.

⑦ **Soviet:** 276th Pipelaying Brigade; 278th Road-Security Brigade.

⑧ **DRA:** 444th Commando Brigade.

⑨ **Soviet:** 177th Motor Rifle Regiment (201st Motor Rifle Division).

⑩ **Soviet:** 22nd Special Forces Brigade.
DRA: 9th Infantry Division.

⑪ **DRA:** 38th Commando Brigade.

⑫ **Soviet:** 45th Engineer-Sapper Regiment.

⑬ **Soviet:** 781st Independent Reconnaissance Battalion; 271st Independent Engineer Sapper Battalion.

⑭ **Soviet:** Divisional HQ, 180th and 181st Motor Rifle Regiments, 1074th Artillery Regiment and 1415th Anti-Aircraft Rocket Regiment (all 108th Motor Rifle Division); 58th Automobile Brigade; 159th (Engineering) Road-Construction Brigade; 264th Independent Special Forces Regiment; 103rd Independent Communications Regiment.
DRA: Army GHQ; I Corps HQ; 15th Armoured Brigade; 37th Commando Brigade; GHQ Artillery Brigade; 99th SAM Regiment.

⑮ **Soviet:** Divisional HQ, 317th and 350th Guards Air Assault Regiments, 1179th Guards Artillery Regiment, 62nd Guards Independent Self-Propelled Artillery Battalion, 130th Guards Independent Engineer-Sapper Battalion and 105th Independent Anti-Aircraft Rocket-Artillery Battalion (all 103rd Guards Air Assault Division).

⑯ **DRA:** 4th Armoured Brigade.

⑰ **Soviet:** 15th Special Forces Brigade; 66th Independent Motor Rifle Brigade.
DRA: 11th Infantry Division; 1st Frontier Brigade.

⑱ **Soviet:** Forward HQ, 40th Army; 357th Guards Air Assault Regiment (103rd Guards Air Assault Division).

⑲ **DRA:** 14th Infantry Division.

⑳ **DRA:** III Corps HQ; 12th Infantry Division.

㉑ **DRA:** 22nd Mountain Brigade.

㉒ **DRA:** 25th Infantry Division; 2nd Frontier Brigade.

㉓ **DRA:** 666th Commando Brigade.

	ANLF	Afghanistan National Liberation Front (Jabha-i-Najat-Milli Afghanistan)
	HI	Islamic Movement (Harakat-i-Islami)
	HIH	Islamic Party of Gulbuddin Hekmatyar (Hizbi Islami (Gulbuddin))
	HIK	Islamic Party of Mawlawi Yunus Khalis (Hizbi Islami (Yunus Khalis))
	IRMA	Islamic Revolutionary Movement (Harakat-i-Inqilab-i-Islami)
	IUA	Islamic Union for the Liberation of Afghanistan (Ittihad-i-Islami)
	IVOA	Islamic Victory Organisation of Afghanistan (Sazman-i-Nasr-i-Islami-yi-Afghanistan)
	JIA	Islamic Society (Jamiat-i-Islami)
	NIFA	National Islamic Front of Afghanistan (Mahaz-i-Milli-Islami)
	RC	Revolutionary Council of the Islamic Union of Afghanistan (Shura-Inqilabi-i-Itifaq-i-Islami)
	Independent fronts	

including MiG-23 and MiG-27 Flogger fighter-bombers, Su-17 and Su-22 Fitter fighter-bombers, plus Tu-16 Badger medium bombers and Su-24 Fencer attack aircraft for bombing missions. Mi-8/Mi-17 Hip helicopters transported troops, ammunition, water and food. Combat helicopters included the Mi-24 Hind attack helicopter, which could provide rapid and accurate firepower for ground attack, convoy escort and patrolling as well as covering troops with close air support. These proved extremely effective against the resistance and were greatly feared. On the other hand, they suffered from vulnerabilities like all weapon systems, and, as helicopters are most exposed when they are on the ground or hovering over a position, the mujahideen tended to achieve reasonable success against such aircraft if they caught them in range while landing or disembarking troops.

DRA forces did not enjoy much respect from their Soviet counterparts – and for good reason. Afghan officers could apply for training in a Soviet military college, sometimes within Afghanistan or occasionally in the Soviet Union itself, but they seldom reached a high standard. Apart from volunteers, ordinary soldiers were often acquired by the crude method of virtual kidnapping: troops entered a village and rounded up men of appropriate age. Exceedingly high rates of desertion, sometimes directly into the ranks of the enemy, and numerous instances of DRA soldiers selling their Soviet-supplied weapons to the resistance – including sometimes tanks and armoured vehicles – did nothing to enhance their appalling reputation. Vladimir Tamarov probably reflected the opinion of many of his comrades when he recorded this disparaging impression:

Frankly, they were lousy soldiers. They tried to stay behind us and were never in a hurry to overtake us. There was nothing surprising about this: many of them, like many of us, were not in this war of their own free will. We had nothing to lose but our lives, but they were fighting their own people on their own land. Our newspapers depicted them as brave and valiant warriors defending their revolution. There were some volunteers who fought on our side to avenge the deaths of their families murdered by the Mujahadeen. Just as there were those who fought on the side of the Mujahadeen to avenge the death of families killed by our shelling. This is what a civil war is about. (Tamarov 2005: 115)

The mujahideen

Resistance fighters tended to avoid direct contact with Soviet forces of superior numbers and firepower lest they risk annihilation. Unlike the Soviets, they very rarely fought from fixed positions and if threatened with encirclement simply withdrew. Similarly, in the grand tradition of guerrilla operations, the mujahideen always sought to achieve advantage through the element of surprise. They benefited enormously from local, intimate knowledge of the ground, possessed years of experience in scouting and reconnaissance-gathering and could transmit intelligence on the movement and strength of Soviet units in rapid fashion and across substantial distances by crude but effective means, including signalling devices that the Soviets could neither interpret nor suppress. The mujahideen were extremely adept at night-fighting, rapid manoeuvre and virtually undetected movement over difficult terrain, and at maintaining a large network of intelligence-gatherers across the country.

Boys as young as eleven or twelve fought, carrying Kalashnikovs, together with their fathers and grandfathers. Their motives were various: in rare exceptions they fought simply for money, but overwhelmingly for the sake of defending their country and affirming tribal loyalty. Whatever other motives existed, without question fighting on behalf of *jihad* or holy war compelled most of them. As one fighter explained to Sandy Gall, a British journalist travelling with the mujahideen:

Jihad embraces the whole Muslim world. All Muslims are obliged to take part in it by sending money, or demonstrating their support in some other way. Any writer or poet should write only about the Jihad. A merchant should work longer hours to make money for the Jihad. Not to take part in Jihad is a sin. (Gall 1988: 1)

A small minority served in the mujahideen out of compulsion: fighters simply arrived at a village and threatened to destroy the houses unless men came forward to serve in their ranks, a process which simultaneously prevented DRA forces from adopting the same practice. The number of mujahideen actively engaged in fighting varied, but an estimated 85,000 served during the final stages of the Soviet occupation in 1988–89.

The mujahid prided himself on exhibiting bravery in action and often demonstrated a careless disregard for his own life. He was highly motivated, functioned on very little food, moved considerable distances on foot without complaint, generally performed great acts of endurance over rough and mountainous terrain, and adopted a fatalistic attitude that rendered him the most formidable of fighting men. John Lee Anderson, an American journalist who accompanied a unit of mujahideen, noted:

Just as they can be harsh when deciding the fate of other people's lives, they can also be stoic when it comes to their own. This stoicism comes out of their culture, in which war enjoys an exalted status, and from their faith in the Islamic idea that after death, a better life awaits. If they are to die, so be it, as long as they do well in battle in the eyes of God. They are mujahideen, holy warriors. They live to make holy war, to kill the enemy, and if necessary be martyred themselves. These are facts they accept.

Members of Jamiat-i-Islami, one of the seven major political resistance factions based in Peshawar, in western Pakistan, which supported their respective mujahideen forces in the field. Led by Professor Burhanuddin Rabbani (1940–2011), Jamiat was among the more moderate fundamentalist groups, with a strong following among the Tajiks, Uzbeks and Turkmens living in Dari-speaking regions. (© Alain Keler/Sygma/Corbis)

Mujahid with an RPG-7, a Soviet-designed grenade launcher. When fired in barrages at close range, they proved effective against modern Soviet tanks as well as infantry fighting vehicles and field entrenchments. The RPG was also used to bring down helicopters. (© Mark Richards/Zuma/Corbis)

Most of them would have it no other way. (Anderson 2006: 148–49)

In true guerrilla fashion, the mujahideen possessed no heavy weapons in the form of aircraft or artillery, and thus depended primarily on small arms. Nevertheless, they did employ heat-seeking, Soviet-made, Egyptian-supplied SAM-7 anti-aircraft missiles, though with very poor results. However, at the end of 1986 the rebels acquired American-made Stingers – rocket launchers used in a ground-to-air target role – as well as Blowpipe missiles. They also possessed recoilless mountain guns, mortars and heavy machine guns, the last known as the DShK, which they pronounced 'Dashika'. Some World War II Soviet weapons passed to the Chinese and thence found their way to Afghanistan. The US purchased and supplied largely Eastern Bloc weapons in order to maintain a policy of deniability,

thereby obviating Soviet retaliation in some form. With the Saudis matching US funds dollar for dollar, and various other donor nations including China, Iran and Britain becoming involved in this illicit arms trade, vast quantities of weapons arrived in Pakistan, where that country's Inter-Service Intelligence (ISI) directly controlled their distribution from near Rawalpindi.

The mujahideen deployed anti-transport mines such as the 7kg Italian-made TS-6.1, as well as anti-personnel mines, some of which popped up and exploded, while others were activated by the vibrations of footsteps or by radio, or set off by mine detectors. The mujahideen discovered mines to be even more effective by planting bombs underneath them to increase the strength of the explosion. Mines of various types were pervasive and sometimes severely impeded the Soviets' movement. As Tamarov explained:

Without minesweepers along, no group ever went into the mountains, no car ever drove off the base, and no transport column ever set out along the road. There were mines everywhere: along the roads, on mountain paths, in abandoned houses. (Tamarov 2005: 74)

Insurgency and intervention

In seeking an understanding of the short-term origins of the Soviet–Afghan War, we must look back 20 months to 27–28 April 1978, when a coup staged by a group of Soviet-trained, largely communist army and air force officers overthrew President Daoud, who had himself come to power by deposing the king, his cousin, in 1973. The king, Zahir Shah, had gone into exile in Italy, while Daoud, who had been prime minister from 1953 to 1963, cultivated close relations with the Soviet Union and introduced communists into the government (about half his cabinet). Soon after taking power, however, Daoud began to change his policies, removed communists from his government and purged leftists from the military. When Daoud's interior minister, Mir Akbar Khyber (1925–78), was murdered on 17 April, a large pro-communist

demonstration occurred in Kabul, prompting Daoud to order the arrest of communist leaders, including Nur Mohammed Taraki, the founder of the party, who was detained on 26 April. The coup began the following day, led in particular by Abdul Qadir Dagarwal (1944–), Mohammad Aslam Watanjar (1946–2000), Sayid Muhammad Gulabzoy (1951–) and Mohammed Rafie (1946–). Rafie and Qadir belonged to the *Parcham* faction of the Afghan communist party, while Gulabzoy and Watanjar came from the *Khalq* wing. Armour under

Nur Mohammed Taraki in May 1978. From the 1930s onwards the Soviets viewed Afghanistan as a state with much potential as a socialist satellite. This ambition reached fruition when in April 1978 Taraki led a communist coup in Kabul against Daoud's republic. (© Kapoor Baldev/Sygma/Corbis)

Watanjar's orders approached the Presidential Palace (known as the *Arg*) with support from MiG-21 fighters and Su-7 fighter-bombers flown from Bagram air base, north of Kabul. The palace guards put up fierce resistance in room-to-room fighting until, at about 4 or 5am on the 28th, the troops reached Daoud and his entire family, whom they murdered. The coup leaders instigated widespread arrests, especially amongst the middle class of Kabul – activists, nationalists and intellectuals – including two former prime ministers. No serious evidence supports the theory that the Soviets inspired the coup, and while KGB officers in the Soviet embassy appear to have known of the plot beforehand they were unenthusiastic about it. Rather, it appears to have been the workings of Afghan communists themselves, though clearly it enjoyed Moscow's blessing, for Soviet advisors in the country immediately offered assistance to the new regime.

The coup leaders soon included key civilian political figures from the People's Democratic Party of Afghanistan (PDPA), with Taraki appointed head of state and prime minister, Hafizullah Amin as foreign minister, Qadir as defence minister and Babrak Karmal as deputy prime minister. In so doing, the regime mixed *Parchami* and *Khalqi* activists, a risky decision that developed into a potentially explosive relationship owing to the fierce antagonism between the two groups. Indeed, within a few months that hostility began to openly emerge. In a meeting on 18 June 1978, which included Taraki, Karmal and others, an argument broke out that resulted in Taraki ordering Karmal out of the room. In an effort to marginalize his influence, Taraki posted Karmal as Afghan ambassador to Czechoslovakia, along with several of his *Parchami* associates. Other *Parchamis* found themselves sent abroad to fill diplomatic posts, and sensibly refused to return home when the Taraki regime redoubled its purge of the *Parcham* faction – including even coup participants like Qadir and Rafie, who probably owed their narrow escape from execution to their Soviet connections.

But many thousands of others enjoyed no such protection and found themselves in the hands of the AGSA (*Afghanistan Gattho Satoonkai Aidara* or Department for Safeguarding the Interests of Afghanistan), the secret police, who imprisoned, tortured and executed thousands in a campaign of terror meant to intimidate real or potential opponents and to consolidate loyalty around the new regime, now dominated by *Khalqis*.

Accordingly, the infamous Pul-e Charkhi prison in Kabul became notorious for mass killings without a semblance of legal proceedings. The PDPA possessed no real ability to rule the country, since owing to political turmoil and repression it neither controlled nor established an experienced state bureaucracy, nor enjoyed widespread support for its ideas and ambitious plans for restructuring the country along Marxist lines. While employing coercion to instil fear proved effective in protecting the regime, the PDPA's failure to govern once it had secured its power base caused considerable uneasiness in Moscow. The *Khalq* movement instituted radical reforms via decree, with wide-ranging land reforms, including the abolition of peasants' debts to landowners, and a drastic widening of women's rights, including freedom of choice in marriage, abolition of bride-price, and compulsory schooling for girls. The extent of the reforms horrified conservative rural sensibilities, in turn encouraging resistance on religious grounds. Gennady Bocharov, a Soviet journalist, eloquently described the disastrous effect caused by functionaries who obtusely believed they could apply Marxist philosophy in the context of a society living almost as it had 500 years earlier:

The revolutionary government reached a revolutionary decision: to give the landowners' property to the peasants.

To the peasants, the revolutionary government was as remote and incomprehensible as a government on another planet. The peasant acknowledges only one authority: the mullah. And mullahs have been saying for hundreds of years that the land belongs to the master. If you

*take so much as a handful of the harvest
without permission, then Allah's wrath is
inescapable. And now this incomprehensible,
distant government is saying – take all the
land, not just a handful of grain.*

*The result was that the land lay untilled.
Unseeded. Land without hands to tend it.
Land running wild …*

*The revolutionary government decided
to introduce co-education in all the schools.*

*Fathers killed daughters who stepped into
a room with boys. Young wives who found
themselves in classrooms with strange young
men had their throats cut by enraged husbands.*

*The authorities in Kabul tried to introduce
a communist subbotnik, or day of voluntary,
unpaid labour, on a Friday, the most important
day of the week for Muslim prayer. Attendance
at the mosques plummeted, resulting in riots.*
(Bocharov 1990: 57)

Even the gradual introduction of such
reforms – including a wide-scale programme
of hospital-building and provision of health
services to the peasantry for the first time –
risked an unpopular reception. In the event,
the rapid pace of change guaranteed a hostile

response to a regime whose representatives,
strangers to the peasantry, journeyed into
the countryside to espouse and implement
radical ideologies, often at great personal
risk. In turn, the regime set upon recalcitrant
villages with pathological heavy-handedness,
creating a vicious cycle of violence and
counter-violence.

Thus, if the new government enjoyed
at least some support amongst the military,
it possessed precious little from amongst
the population as a whole, most of which
consisted of small-holding peasant farmers,
on behalf of whom the coup leaders
instigated the revolution. By painful
irony, the peasants in particular – but some
workers, too – rejected the call to Marxism
and across the country fomented armed
resistance. This movement was encouraged
by the poor combat-readiness of DRA forces,

Mujahideen formed in the early days of resistance.
The war in Afghanistan did not constitute a national
movement, but nevertheless the rural population
castigated the Soviets as atheistic, foreign occupiers
seeking to implement reforms utterly abhorrent to an
essentially reactionary society. (© Reza/Webistan/Corbis)

which were reeling from a wave of bloody officer purges that together with large-scale desertions rapidly reduced the officer corps to half its normal complement. Some personnel from the lower ranks also abandoned their units, either returning home or joining the resistance, taking their arms and skills with them. But Taraki remained ideologically unshaken; indeed, he strengthened his ties with the Soviet Union when on 5 December 1978 his government signed a treaty that provided for further economic and military aid from Moscow and a 20-year period of 'friendship and co-operation' between the two countries. When barely a year later the Soviets invaded Afghanistan they cited the terms of military co-operation stipulated in Article 4 as justifying their action. The treaty thus represented a further overt Soviet effort to bind Afghanistan within its sphere of influence, with military intervention now implicit as a guarantor of fidelity.

On 15 March 1979, owing to brutality committed by *Khalq* activists, a mass revolt erupted in the western city of Herat. Most of the Afghan 17th Division joined the rebel cause, slaughtering untold numbers of government officials as well as some Soviet advisors, who numbered about 550 across the country by this time, and their families. Units loyal to the government moved against Herat and eventually occupied it while the air force bombed the city and the 17th Division. A staggering 5,000 civilians are believed to have died in the onslaught. This extremely brutal approach by the regime made many other soldiers desert to the resistance, some as individuals but others as entire units and even entire brigades, reducing army strength by the end of the year to less than half its official strength of 90,000 personnel.

The riots and massacre in Herat triggered an uprising across whole swathes of the country, with opposition preached by mosques and village elders who condemned Marxism as atheistic and anti-Muslim. Religious leaders declared a jihad, and as fighting spread across the country the disruption of government business and the

harassment of army units and state officials by the mujahideen rapidly amounted to an intractable problem. Over succeeding months, as the resistance movement gathered pace, there appeared some prospect of its actually overthrowing the regime, reversing the communist revolution and installing an Islamic government in Kabul. In light of the Islamic revolutionary movement's recent ascent to power under the Ayatollah Khomeini (1900–89) in Iran, immediately to the west of Afghanistan, the Soviets naturally wished to prevent this eventuality, not least because of the obvious threat posed to the key principle underpinning the Brezhnev Doctrine: that once communism achieved a foothold in government, the process became irreversible. To the USSR, any instance of a Marxist 'roll-back' anywhere in the world was anathema on grounds of the potential precedent it set for Eastern Europe, not to mention the Soviet republics themselves.

The Herat uprising caused a serious degree of alarm in Moscow, which began to pay closer attention to military and political events in Afghanistan. If Taraki managed to maintain his grip on power, the Soviet Union could rest fairly easily with a friendly satellite state on its southern borders, a state of affairs critically important in light of the USSR's Muslim republics (Turkmenistan, Uzbekistan and Tajikistan) situated there. Leonid Brezhnev, the Soviet leader, feared that unrest in Afghanistan could spread elsewhere in Central Asia, so threatening the territorial integrity of the USSR. On 17 March the Soviet Foreign Minister, Andrei Gromyko (1909–89), argued to the Politburo that Afghanistan must not fall from the Soviet orbit, while Aleksei Kosygin, Chairman of the Council of Ministers and later a successor to Gromyko in the Foreign Ministry, stated that the Afghan regime was dangerously inflaming internal opposition and actively attempting to conceal its wide-scale acts of repression from the Soviets. Taraki hysterically and repeatedly requested the intervention of Soviet troops to help maintain order in

Afghanistan, but when Kosygin met with him in Moscow on 20 March to outline the Soviet position on Afghan internal affairs, he refused direct military aid: Soviet intervention would worsen matters by inflaming opposition to the regime and arousing international condemnation. The meeting suggests that the Soviets contemplated no long-term strategy to wage war in Afghanistan; it is therefore instructive to examine how and why the Kremlin's *volte face* occurred between March and December 1979.

Matters shifted radically in Afghan politics when in September Taraki and his prime minister, Hafizullah Amin, fell out. The latter, suspecting that Taraki and the Soviets were plotting to oust him, seized Taraki and had him executed on the 14th. This untimely development did not please the Soviets and Brezhnev in particular, who was affronted by his protégé's demise under Amin's orders. Significantly, the coup led to nothing less than a fundamental shift in the USSR's attitude and foreign policy respecting its southern neighbour, with the relationship between the two beginning to deteriorate so rapidly that the notion of a Soviet invasion

Afghan students in Kabul demonstrate against the Soviet invasion, January 1980. Opposition to communist rule had already begun throughout the country after Taraki's coup in April 1978 and carried on after his replacement by Amin five months later. It grew apace with the Soviets' fixture of Karmal in power from December 1979 and through Najibullah's regime, which ended in 1992. (© Bettmann/Corbis)

began from this point to become a viable option for the Kremlin.

In the event, Amin's reign of terror – led by the KhAD (*Khedamat-e Ettelaat-e Dawlati* or State Intelligence Agency), as the AGSA was now called – proved worse than Taraki's, with the ruthless pursuit of thousands of genuine and perceived dissidents appearing to be the only answer to Amin's failure to stabilize the domestic situation. The Soviets, angered that this merely exacerbated Amin's internal woes, distanced themselves from his regime, leaving him with no hope of developing closer relations with other powers such as the United States; the US looked particularly unfavourably at the regime after February, when its security forces botched a rescue attempt to recover the US ambassador in Kabul from the hands of unidentified kidnappers. Besides,

Mounted resistance fighters near Herat, January 1980 – the year after the rebellion and massacre that helped push Moscow towards intervention. The invasion of a remote and little-known country did not simply expose the inadequacies of the Soviet military machine to cope with a virulent insurgency, but played an important role in the process that eventually toppled the Soviet state itself. (© Bettmann/Corbis)

the United States, under President Jimmy Carter, found itself so diverted by events in Iran (on 4 November revolutionaries had seized the entire American diplomatic corps from the US Embassy in Tehran) that it paid little attention to Amin's predicament.

Thus, by the autumn of 1979, with the Afghan economy in a downward spiral, the regime rent by political infighting, the country racked by full-fledged civil war and the mujahideen's increasingly effective opposition looking certain to end in Amin's downfall, the Soviets felt compelled to act. In the months prior to the invasion, Soviet military and KGB advisors toured the country under various pretences to determine the best method of ensuring a rapid subjugation of the country with a minimum of interference from Afghan forces. But the actual decision to invade did not apparently come until 12 December, during a meeting of the Politburo chaired by Gromyko and

attended by Party General Secretary Brezhnev, Andropov, the KGB chairman, and the defence minister, Dmitriy Ustinov (1908–84). The first deployments appear to have begun when the 105th Guards Air Assault Division, under Marshal Sergei Sokolov (1911–), shifted troops from Termez in Uzbekistan to Bagram air base, north of Kabul, beginning on 29 November. Late on the evening of 24 December, further contingents from the 105th set down at the civilian airport in Kabul, while other units arrived via heavy Ilyushin and Antonov transport planes at Bagram, the air base at Shindand near Herat, and at Kandahar, the last of the major airfields in the country. In addition, units of the 360th Motor Rifle Division crossed the border near Termez *en route* to the Afghan capital. By launching the invasion around Christmas, the Soviets hoped to lessen the likelihood of any concerted Western objection. Government troops offered no resistance, since they believed the arrival of Soviet forces represented Moscow's desire to uphold Amin in power. As a precaution, Soviet advisors had already removed the firing mechanisms from large numbers of Afghan tanks on the spurious ground that the machines required 'winterizing'.

A war without fronts

While the Soviet–Afghan War may be divided into distinct phases by historians, it is vital to appreciate that the nature of insurgency defies strict adherence to convenient divisions. Set-piece battles, distinct campaigns and decisive actions indicating the conflict's changing course seldom if ever occur in asymmetric warfare. It is in the very nature of an insurgency, characterized by low- and medium-intensity fighting and the enormous disparity between the protagonists' capabilities, that neither side is capable of inflicting a decisive blow on its opponent via clear-cut encounters. As with all unconventional conflicts, the outcome of the Soviet–Afghan War would depend upon the cumulative effect of years of steadily applied combat power in an attritional contest, in which the winner succeeded in grinding down his opponent through unacceptable losses and a broken will.

Before briefly examining the operational phases of the war a concise discussion of the basic nature of the fighting may be instructive. From the outset fighting took place throughout Afghanistan, with the highest pitch reached in the east, a fact confirmed by the large proportion of refugees and internally displaced Afghans who fled

DRA head of state Babrak Karmal, depicted in January 1980. In the course of their invasion the Soviets installed Karmal in the hope that his regime would acquire respectability and thus ostensibly represent a genuine national government, although one transparently closely connected with the Soviet Union. His attempts to recover support by replacing the red flag with the old three-coloured national version, granting state salaries to thousands of Muslim leaders and providing public money to build mosques failed to placate dissent and he left office under Soviet pressure on 5 May 1986, ostensibly on health grounds. (© Henri Bureau/Sygma/Corbis)

Jubilant fighters standing on a destroyed Mi-8 Hip-E attack helicopter in Kunar province, January 1980. The resistance hated and feared such machines more than any other form of weaponry the Soviets brought to bear, particularly the Mi-24 Hind attack helicopter, which was used for close air support, escorting convoys, patrolling, and bombing villages. Capable of operating both during the day and at night, the Hind was heavily armoured and difficult to bring down. Armed with an under-nose 12.7mm machine gun, it also carried 57mm rocket pods, incendiary pods, cluster bomb units, a twin-barrelled cannon, and high-explosive and white phosphorus bombs. (© Alain Dejean/Sygma/Corbis)

the area over the course of the nine-year conflict. As this region adjoined the Pakistani border, across which the bulk of foreign aid flowed to the resistance over this period, the country's eastern provinces naturally became the focus of particular Soviet attention, with the establishment of a buffer or *cordon sanitaire* their principal objective. To that end, the normal course of fighting served well in encouraging or forcing civilians to abandon the region for the safety and refuge provided by nearby Pakistan. Only later did the Soviets institute a deliberate policy of de-populating vast stretches of territory in a bid to deny the mujahideen local support in various forms, including food, shelter and basic intelligence. From the beginning of the war and for most of its course, the majority of the operations conducted by the resistance remained consistent with their limited offensive capacity. These consisted of a series of small-scale (albeit seemingly relentless) attacks conducted across most parts of country – the central region of the Hazarajat figuring as a notable exception – in the form of raids, hit-and-run attacks and moderately sized strikes against Soviet and Afghan regime bases, reconnaissance parties and small convoys. Bocharov described one such attack against a column of armoured personnel carriers:

He clambered out of a hole and opened up with a grenade launcher. The first shot ricocheted off Nikolai's APC and exploded a little way ahead. The next one hit the turret dead-on …

Notwithstanding their martial prowess, the mujahideen lacked an overall strategy and failed to co-ordinate their small, independently executed attacks. The men in any given region did not fight for the liberation of their country or to achieve some national goal, but rather pursued the interests of their own respective region and individual families. (© Les Stone/Sygma/Corbis)

Another missile went under the front wheels and exploded below the first axle. A searing flame burst through from under Nikolai's seat. He felt his entire back to be on fire …

He rolled out onto the body of the vehicle – awful, awful – everything burning all around, no sign of any of the others, just the chatter of automatic fire. He fell to the ground just as two missiles turned the APC into a useless heap of metal. (Bocharov 1990: 36–37)

Two further APCs were hit, killing and wounding several soldiers. Then support arrived in the form of Mi-24 helicopters:

The choppers swooped over the line of foxholes … spitting out pinkish-blue streaks of fire and missiles. Mud, sand, and rocks fountained up, showered down on the trenches, and obscured the sky. The earth groaned with explosions and gave birth to dead men'. (Bocharov 1990: 40–41)

The mujahideen proved masters at launching such attacks from places of concealment, as Bocharov again recounts:

Attacks on Soviet armoured groups were usually carried out without any prior warning. The spooks would emerge out of camouflaged manholes and open fire. Then they would disappear into the depths of their 'kirizes', a network of underground tunnels dug for irrigation purposes, but now serving as perfect bolt holes… They stretched under fields, alongside roads, and underneath villages. Kirizes under villages drove the Soviet soldiers mad. One minute you'd have concentrated fire coming from a village, but when you entered it, there wouldn't be a soul to be seen: everyone would have gone to ground in the kirizes, and the village would be deserted. (Bocharov 1990: 35–36)

However, these examples should not assert that the Soviet–Afghan War must only be seen in the light of elusive guerrilla attacks followed in their wake by the hammer-blows of a superpower wielding numerically superior numbers and advanced technology, for the resistance did not always hold the initiative. Indeed, as early as March 1980 the Soviets launched their first major offensive with a sweep through the Kunar Valley, which left approximately a thousand mujahideen and Afghan civilians dead, yet achieved little more than temporarily driving out to other valleys resistance leaders who, in the wake of imminent Soviet withdrawal, resumed their initial positions. Indeed, this scenario strongly characterized the course of the war. The Soviets applied overwhelming force to enable ground troops to establish temporary control of an area after inflicting perhaps sizeable, but seldom crushing and therefore meaningful, casualties on the enemy. These ground troops would then be withdrawn with only a small (and therefore a vulnerable) or no presence left behind, enabling those same opponents to re-establish their former presence over territory that Soviet and/or regime forces would have to clear again – a frustrating and costly affair that inevitably favoured the insurgency.

Much of the fighting involved insurgent ambushes directed against patrols and convoys. In the case of the former, the mujahideen possessed better knowledge of the ground and often struck under cover of darkness, while in the case of the latter, they took full advantage of the limited routes available to Soviet and government forces, who found their freedom of movement, even over short distances, hampered by a shortage of roads, particularly paved ones. Regular troops, not trained to confront opponents operating according to radically different doctrine, tactics, and methods of supply and evacuation, could not hope to proceed across hundreds of miles of trackless, often mountainous, ground without commensurate support in terms of air power, artillery and supply. Thus, large formations necessarily depended upon the existing network of rudimentary roads –

ironically, most of these constructed by fellow Soviets since World War II.

From the Soviet point of view, the war may be divided into four phases: the first involving invasion and consolidation from December 1979 to February 1980; the second, characterized by the Soviets' elusive pursuit of victory between March 1980 and April 1985; the third constituting the period of fighting at its height from May 1985 to December 1986; and the fourth represented by the period of withdrawal from November 1986 to February 1989. These will be examined in turn.

Phase One: December 1979–February 1980

The Soviet invasion amounted to a *coup de main* employing a strategy modelled on that used in their last cross-border intervention during a period of unrest (Czechoslovakia in the spring of 1968). Hostilities began in Kabul on 27 December, when air assault and Spetsnaz forces seized the vital Salang Tunnel and key government and communications points in the capital. There Colonel Grigori Boyarinov (1922–79), leading special forces, specifically sought out Amin, who had recently relocated from the *Arg* to the Tajbeg Palace in the southern part of the capital. There the Soviet assault force surrounded and stormed the building, killing Amin and most of his family, but losing Boyarinov in the process. During the assault the city's telephone system shut down after a deliberately timed explosion, and on the evening of the 28th the Soviets used a powerful radio transmitter on their own soil to broadcast a recording of Babrak Karmal announcing Amin's overthrow and naming himself successor. As far as the Soviets were concerned, their seizure of key points across the country, together with the successful installation of Karmal in power, ought to have signalled the practical end of their major military operations in Afghanistan.

Soviet strategy concentrated on a few key objectives. First, the army was to bring stability to the country by protecting the main thoroughfares, placing large garrisons in the major cities, and guarding air bases and points of logistical significance. Once ensconced in these positions, Soviet troops planned to relieve Afghan government forces of garrison duties and redirect DRA efforts against the resistance in rural areas, where the Soviets would provide support on a number of fronts: logistics, intelligence, air power and artillery. This would enable Soviet forces to take a secondary role in the fighting, thereby both minimizing their contact with the Afghan population and keeping their casualties to an acceptable level. Finally, they planned to strengthen Afghan government forces to the extent that once resistance ceased the Soviets could withdraw their own troops and leave governance and security matters to the 'puppet' regime left in their wake.

The fact that the occupying forces did not anticipate serious resistance may be discerned from their original rules of engagement, which specified that troops were only to return fire if attacked, or to rescue Soviet advisors in insurgent hands. By necessity, these rules rapidly came to be altered owing to the rise in casualties from the very beginning, not least those sustained from urban unrest, the worst of which occurred on 21 February 1980 when approximately 300,000 people crowded the streets of Kabul shouting anti-government and anti-Soviet slogans. The demonstrations continued into the following day when the crowds flowed into the main streets and squares and appeared before the *Arg*, where Karmal made his residence. Thousands laid siege to government buildings, threw projectiles at the Soviet Embassy and killed several Soviet citizens. After the rioters looted scores of shops, overturned and burned cars and set ablaze a hotel, General Yuri Tukharinov, commander of the 40th Army, received orders to block the main approaches to Kabul and stop the demonstrations. This he achieved, but the rising in the capital marked the proper beginning of a resistance movement now extending its remit to

Soviet soldiers surrounded by artillery casings. Uniforms furnished to Soviet troops in Afghanistan were of the camouflage pattern designed for northern Europe, and thus totally inappropriate. Boots meant for use in Europe generated too much noise over Afghan terrain and did not function well in the mountains. Similarly, rucksacks, of 1950s design, were not designed to carry heavy loads over substantial distances or for continuous use beyond the protection afforded by an armoured personnel carrier. (© Patrick Robert/Sygma/Corbis)

foreign forces acting on behalf of Karmal's illegitimate regime.

This left the 40th Army with the unenviable task of defeating the insurgency across the country, a task for which, owing to its original remit of the previous December, it was not properly equipped or trained. In the course of this first phase of the war, that is, the two months from the end of December 1979 to the end of February 1980, the 40th Army had already suffered 245 fatal casualties, largely attributable to regular attacks launched against columns of troops and supplies on the main roads from the Soviet Union. The army responded by establishing mutually supporting guard posts (*zastavas*) at regular intervals that secured the main

Soviet armoured personnel carriers, either BTR-60PBs or BTR-70s, in front of the Darulaman Palace in Kabul, January 1980. The Soviet plan of invasion bore the hallmarks of those employed in Hungary and Czechoslovakia in 1956 and 1968, respectively. Air assault and Spetsnaz forces would spearhead the invasion and capture major airfields, key points of transportation, the more important government ministries in Kabul and communications centres. After arresting or killing the principal government figures, Soviet ground forces would enter the country and occupy the major cities. (© Henri Bureau/Sygma/Corbis)

roads, principal cities, airports, bridges, power stations and pipelines. These posts observed the insurgents' movements, supported convoy escorts, and could call in air or artillery strikes as necessary. By the end of February 1980, 862 *zastavas* dotted the landscape, scattered across Afghanistan, containing garrisons amounting in total to more than 20,000 troops, a fifth of the 40th Army's manpower. This committed troops to a necessary yet static function when the Soviets required substantial numbers actually to pursue and engage the insurgents in order to maintain the initiative or at least to deny it to the enemy. General Valentin Varennikov (1923–2009), deputy chief of the Soviet General Staff during the conflict, described one *zastava*, situated on the apex of a mountain near Kabul:

The territory of the zastava was shaped like an irregular rectangle. On three sides it was surrounded by a solid wall of sandbags brought in by helicopter. There was no fourth wall, because it was here the helicopter would touch down with one 'foot' on the land. There were two heavy DShK machine guns at either end of this square, which was about 6 square metres in area. Steps led down to a little square below. Here there was a 120mm mortar, with a mountain of shells piled up beside it, and a shelter from the weather.

From the little square, a path ran downwards at about 45 [degrees], a set of steps hacked out of the granite rock, on both sides of which was stretched a stout rope instead of banisters. At the bottom there was another little square, about the same size as the one above. Here there was another heavy machine gun and this was where the tiny garrison – 12 men in all – had their living; a place to relax, a kitchen, somewhere to wash and so on, the furniture – chairs, tables, sleeping places – all made out of ammunition boxes. (Quoted in Braithwaite 2011: 141)

Mujahideen. By nature they preferred noisy, direct attacks that brought them into close contact with Soviet and DRA targets, as opposed to acts of sabotage against oil or gas pipelines or other vital facilities. In this respect they declined to execute such potentially devastating operations as planting truck bombs in the Salang Tunnel, much to the disappointment of the ISI and the CIA, who hoped to broaden the role of the resistance into something akin to that performed by the British Special Operations Executive during World War II. (© Pascal Manoukian/Sygma/Corbis)

Phase Two:
March 1980–April 1985

During this period both the 40th Army and the mujahideen modified their tactics in light of the painful lessons already drawn from the first two months of conflict. No longer would the resistance take on the Soviets in direct confrontations; instead, they turned to guerrilla tactics, with frequent, often small-scale hit-and-run attacks against outposts, convoys and small units, always seeking to employ the advantage of surprise, particularly in the context of an ambush. The insurgents also planted booby traps and mines along frequently travelled patrol and convoy routes, as well as in abandoned villages. However, the Soviets could sometimes play the game, too, laying ambushes along their opponents' supply routes, as Bocharov witnessed:

A spray of bullets punctured the camels' bellies and brought them to the ground, clumsily, onto their fore-legs, roaring with pain. One camel flipped over completely and skidded along the sand on its hump and the boxes strapped to it. The spooks, robbed of cover, sprinted in different directions. One escaped, but they got the other one. Bullets raked through his pelvis just as he got to the lip of the ravine. (Bocharov 1990: 24)

Still, more often than not it was the Soviets who were ambushed in this way, and to compound their already formidable problems the mujahideen became increasingly ingenious in their methods of laying mines, as Bocharov recalled respecting an APC moving between Bagram and Kabul:

They bypassed the combined anti-tank and anti-personnel minefields, and negotiated the most dangerous spot ... without incident. Two stray rocket missiles whistled by harmlessly. On one of the sharp turns, the telescopic antenna that cut through the air above the APC slashed a branch of an overhanging tree. A deafening explosion echoed around the valley, sending stabs of pain through the soldiers'

eardrums. Despite its weight of many tons, the APC was flung forward like an empty tub ...

There had been a mine fixed to the tree branch, and the antenna had hit it, setting it off. The mine had been put there with APC radio antennas in mind: they were long and flexible, striking branches and rocky overhangs on the mountain roads. (Bocharov 1990: 32)

But the resistance did not rely exclusively on the remote actions of their explosive devices, however numerous and cleverly planted or laid. They supplemented these measures with audacious attacks, as when in the summer of 1980 they bombarded the 40th Army's headquarters, less than 7km (4½ miles) from Kabul, with rockets. The Soviets did not remain idle, striking at resistance positions that they often located from the air and launching the first of many large-scale operations, notably full-scale sweeps of the Kunar and Panjshir valleys between February and April 1980. The last of these marked the largest single Soviet operation since 1945. This dislodged insurgents from a wide area, but only temporarily, while smaller units left themselves vulnerable to mujahideen attacks of their own, such as in August when the 783rd Independent Reconnaissance Battalion of the 201st Motor Rifle Division fell into an ambush at Kisham in Badakhshan province, near the frontier with Tajikistan, and lost 45 men.

The Soviets struck again in the Panjshir Valley in September 1980, followed by other sweeps against guerrillas in November and from January to February 1981. This region, northeast of Kabul, held particular strategic significance owing to its proximity to the road running north–south that connected Kabul and Mazar-e Sharif through the Salang Tunnel and Pul-e Khumri in Baghlan province. This represented the stronghold of Ahmad Shah Massoud (1953–2001), the best-known mujahideen leader to emerge during the war. Soviet and DRA forces made nine substantial efforts to clear and hold the Panjshir but never succeeded. Other sizeable operations in 1981 included a largely DRA offensive, which succeeded in securing the Kabul–Jalalabad road near Sarowbi in Kabul province in July. However, regime forces suffered from low morale, performed poorly, and depended heavily on Soviet co-operation, or shamelessly left the execution of major operations entirely

Right: Ahmed Shah Massoud, a Tajik and former engineering student, is depicted here in June 1985. He made his stronghold in the Panjshir Valley in the Nuristan region in north-central Afghanistan. Five 15,000ft passes cut through Panjshir, which means 'Valley of Five Lions' in Persian. (© Reza/Webistan/Corbis)

Below: Aerial view of the Panjshir Valley, the scene of numerous unsuccessful Soviet attempts to clear out mujahideen strongholds and troop concentrations. Topography like this, amongst other factors, has historically defied efforts to unify Afghanistan into a sovereign state, as it is a loose collection of tribes and ethnic groups over which, for many centuries, central governments have seldom exercised more than a moderate degree of influence, much less actual control. (© Reza/Webistan/Corbis)

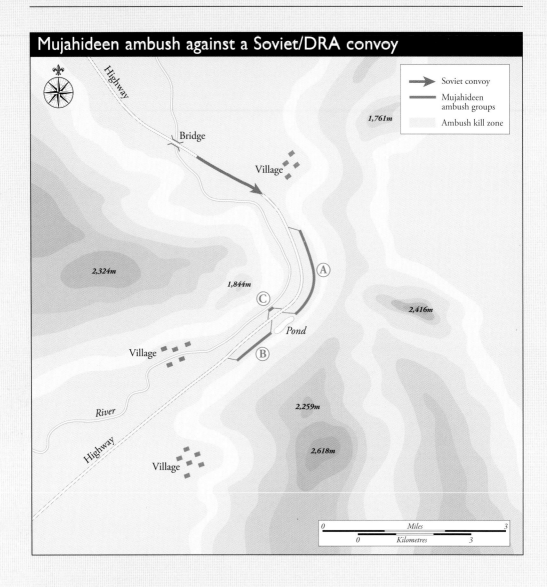

Mujahideen ambush against a Soviet/DRA convoy

to their patrons. This policy applied equally to the Soviets' fourth major offensive into the Panjshir Valley, in August. This, like the others before it, failed, largely owing to paltry troop levels that rendered holding ground all but impossible for any substantial period. As before, the resistance simply re-established itself across the ground from which the Soviets had temporarily driven it by dint of superior firepower. Resistance casualties certainly mounted, but replacements were always to be found amongst those driven from villages

destroyed from the air, living in squalid refugee camps over the border, or preparing for jihad in one of the hundreds of *madrassas* (religious schools) in Pakistan, whence thousands of displaced Afghans joined the resistance with the promise of martyrdom for those killed in their holy cause.

In the west, around Herat, Soviet and regime forces engaged in heavy fighting with the mujahideen in October 1981, with the air base at Shindand, south of Herat, the strong focus of resistance attention. Such actions proved that, despite inhospitable terrain

One of the most common tactics employed by the mujahideen was the ambush, by which they made best use of choke-points and high ground to concentrate their forces, strike a target made vulnerable by confined space and poor fire zones, disable or destroy a convoy, seize provisions and retreat before heliborne forces could arrive to support the defenders. In this theoretical scenario, mujahideen execute an ambush against a convoy of trucks. Such attacks disrupted Soviet and DRA forces' resupply and tied up troops otherwise deployed on strike operations.

This scenario, taking place at about 1pm on a July day, shows a force of mujahideen setting an ambush against a supply column of 48 trucks, accompanied by an escorting BTR-70 APC at the front and another at the rear; each BTR-70 has a 14.5mm heavy machine gun as its main armament plus a coaxial 7.62mm machine gun, and carries a detachment of seven motor-rifle infantrymen in addition to the three-man crew. The column is moving along a paved section of the 'ring road' linking Afghanistan's major cities and points of supply; the highway is skirted by a river and running through a gorge. The trucks are travelling at 100m intervals; they are carrying food, fuel, oil and lubricants, and ammunition to areas beyond the reach of the supply pipelines upon which the Soviets and their DRA allies depended. The ambush site is located at a particularly vulnerable choke-point where the river runs close to the highway and the hills rise sharply, rendering escape problematical for the convoy's personnel.

The 112-man attacking force is divided into three groups. One group (**A**), 45 men-strong with two RPGs and deployed along the bend, is meant to engage the centre of the convoy and the rearguard APC. Another (**B**), also 45 men strong but with three RPGs, is to engage the advanced guard and the van of the convoy. A third group (**C**), 22 men with a single RPG, is sequestered in ruined houses beside the river they are taking advantage of natural cover that happens to be on the west side of the road and can help bring fire down on any enemy personnel who, perceiving the heaviest fire coming from the east, are likely to exit their vehicles and try to use them for cover. The overall commander is with Group B; none of the groups has radio communication with the other two. The fighters are armed with AK-47 Kalashnikov assault rifles, a few bolt-action Enfield rifles and six RPG-7s, and are hidden in ditches not visible from the road, in concealed positions employing camouflage netting and low-growing vegetation on high ground, or in the ruins.

Based on knowledge of the convoy's time of departure and an appreciation of the average speed of a convoy's progress based on previous experience, the mujahideen commander has made a rough calculation of the convoy's arrival at a given point along its route. His force will attack when the end of the column reaches the northernmost point of Group A's position. Advance warning of the convoy's approach is made available by spotters in the town of the convoy's origin, with the estimated time of arrival in the gorge anticipated with a fair degree of accuracy even without radio communication.

Surprise is likely to reap excellent results: RPGs fired at close range will destroy the APCs to front and rear; the fuel tankers, vulnerable to small-arms fire and grenades, will be attacked and blown up; and the remaining vehicles, carrying food and ammunition, will be stripped of their loads, with any intact trucks driven away to a mujahideen concentration area – likely to be close by, as Soviet-built trucks could not usually operate off road. After setting all damaged vehicles on fire and stripping the enemy dead of their personal weapons, the mujahideen will promptly leave the area, aware that helicopters will soon arrive to ferry away the Soviet/DRA dead and any wounded.

and the great distances across which they conveyed supplies by mule, donkey, camel and packhorse through the treacherous passes connecting Afghanistan with Pakistan, the mujahideen could still undertake operations frequently and on a respectable scale. This circumstance was partly rendered feasible by the large exodus of residents from Herat, who were appalled by the regime's suppression of the rising of March 1979 and consequently drawn to the anti-Soviet cause. Further major encounters in and around Herat between the resistance and Soviet and Afghan forces took place in December 1981 and into January of the following year, with continuous, low-level fighting occurring thereafter.

The Afghan regime's ineptitude came to the fore in April 1982 when mujahideen penetrated Bagram air base and destroyed 23 Soviet and Afghan Air Force aircraft. The following month, another major Soviet–Afghan offensive into the Panjshir occurred, followed by another in August and September, perhaps the largest of all the nine conducted in that area. Both failed to make inroads against Massoud's strongholds despite the enormous scale of the operations. As a consequence of the stalemate reached there, the regime negotiated a ceasefire with Massoud that held from December 1982 to April 1984 on what appeared mutually beneficial terms, enabling the Soviets to release thousands of their troops for potentially more successful operations elsewhere. The ceasefire simultaneously provided some relief to Massoud's exhausted forces, and particularly to the gravely stricken local population, whose humanitarian needs the insurgents could not adequately meet in the midst of the Soviet offensive, especially when compounded by the severe winter of 1982–83. Moreover, Massoud's forces had suffered heavily during the offensive, and the ceasefire probably enabled him to recover and regroup before pursuing new operations further north, such as in the Shomali Valley, north of Kabul, where it is thought he struck,

Soviet Mi-8 Hip-E attack helicopters landing at Faisabad Airport. Whereas tanks proved of limited value, helicopters served the indispensable roles of rapid troop insertion and extraction, supply, evacuation of the wounded and, of course, firepower. (© Reza/Webistan/Corbis)

in conjunction with other commanders, at Soviet positions near Balkh.

In 1983 the Soviets altered their strategy fundamentally, embarking on a deliberate policy of clearing the Afghan population from rural areas and driving them either to seek refuge in the cities, where Soviet or DRA forces exercised more or less total control, or to other, less strategically vital areas within the country or over the border into Iran (which particularly sympathized with and armed the Shi'a minority in Afghanistan) or Pakistan. At the same time, the Soviets continued to conduct major operations against areas where the resistance appeared in concentrated numbers, a painstaking, exhausting and frequently fruitless undertaking. Owing to poor intelligence, they often directed the focus of their attention in the wrong area of the country, as in the case of the north in the spring of 1983. Here Abdul Qader, known more commonly by his *nom de guerre*, Zabiullah, led as many as 20,000 men and continued to conduct the sort of small-scale operations initiated by him three years before, including attacks, raids and ambushes in Baghlan, Balkh and Kunduz provinces, all north or northwest of Kabul. Amongst

numerous mujahideen successes during this phase of the war, the victory achieved in May in Mazar-e Sharif, the principal city of northern Afghanistan, figured prominently. Mazar-e Sharif, whose flat and treeless surroundings rendered guerrilla operations particularly difficult, nevertheless witnessed a bold mujahideen attack that brought down the civilian airport's control tower.

As was common throughout the country, Zabiullah operated with other local, albeit less powerful, commanders who vied for control of their respective immediate areas, or indeed tried to lay claim to territory well beyond their normal areas of operation. It is vital to appreciate that the mujahideen did not operate as a unified fighting force with any common objective beyond that of ousting the Soviets from Afghan soil and overthrowing the communist regime, whether headed by Taraki or Amin before the Soviets arrived, or Karmal or Najibullah thereafter. Rivalry between different mujahideen units, which could consist of merely a dozen to several thousand fighters, sometimes led to open feuds over contested ground; indeed, observers did not rule out the fact that Zabiullah's death, caused by a mine in December 1984, may have constituted assassination rather than a simple vagary of war. If commanders could agree on a common foreign enemy, they still maintained an eye on Afghanistan's long-term political future and their place in it.

During the course of 1984, in line with their policy of depopulating regions presumed sympathetic to the mujahideen, the Soviets conducted a wide-scale bombing campaign in the west, particularly around Herat, driving untold thousands across the border into nearby Iran. In the Panjshir Valley, with the ceasefire over in April, the Soviets opened yet another major offensive that continued into May, with another following in September. The Soviets again employed their new strategy of depopulation through a combination of intensive shell fire, regular bombing raids, and mine-laying.

Upon returning from a visit to Afghanistan in 1983, Congressman Charles Wilson, from Texas, began to champion the cause of the mujahideen 'freedom-fighters' and aggressively lobbied the Reagan administration to aid their cause. As a member of the Defense Appropriations Subcommittee, responsible for funding CIA operations, Wilson secured billions of dollars for the procurement of weapons, all covertly supplied to the resistance via the Pakistani intelligence service, the ISI. (© Bettmann/Corbis)

In August, the Soviets sought to relieve the siege of the garrison at Ali Sher in Paktia province. There followed further efforts against the resistance in the east from January 1985, with the purpose of clearing areas in order to create bases along the Pakistani border, both to interdict the movement of supplies into Afghanistan and to weaken the flow of resistance fighters seeking a temporary safe haven in the tribal areas of western Pakistan or in that country's province of Baluchistan further to the south. During this second phase, which ended in April 1985, the Soviets suffered 9,175 fatal casualties – an average of 148 per month.

Phase Three: May 1985–December 1986

During this period Gorbachev, who came to power in March 1985, opened negotiations in an effort to withdraw Soviet forces while

A column of mujahideen marches through the snow. They conducted the majority of their operations in the warmer months, trailing off as winter approached. During cold periods some mujahideen sought refuge in Pakistan or left the relatively protective isolation of the mountains in search of accommodation in the villages. Although their assaults decreased in winter, they occasionally attacked convoys carrying weapons, ammunition and food arriving from the Soviet Union, even when snow seriously impeded their operations. (© Pascal Manoukian/Sygma/Corbis)

simultaneously attempting to reduce the level of casualties during a period when discontent with the war steadily grew. Soviet troops sought increasingly to pass responsibility for making hostile contact with the resistance to their Afghan regime allies; depending themselves more on air and artillery operations; and employing motor-rifle units to support DRA forces both operationally and in terms of morale. As Soviet and Afghan government forces continued to struggle in the east of the country, in June 1985 the resistance struck Shindand air base in the west, destroying about 20 aircraft. Fighting in nearby Herat in July grew so intense that the governor was obliged to leave the city, while at the same time the Soviets launched their ninth and last major offensive in the Panjshir Valley. The DRA regime also continued its efforts: in January 1986 its forces attacked Zendejan in Herat province, inflicting heavy casualties on resistance elements but failing to consolidate their own tenuous control over the region. In the spring, anticipating a Soviet offensive against Zhawar in Paktia province, near the Pakistani border, the mujahideen reinforced their base there, strengthening their anti-aircraft positions and placing them about 7km (4½ miles) outside their base, complete with defences in depth. They mined the approaches, while small arms, RPGs, mortars and recoilless rifles covered the area. Communications in the form of field telephones and radios kept the various outposts in contact with one another. The Soviets, in turn, provided one regiment of air assault troops together with 12,000 DRA personnel. Only 800 mujahideen

defended the base at Zhawar, but they received advanced warning of the attack by the presence of two waves of helicopters that approached ahead of the main assault. Air strikes and an artillery bombardment followed, though the attackers could not be certain of the insurgents' positions.

At 7am heliborne troops touched down at scattered landing zones near Zhawar.

Ahmed Shah Massoud training his troops in May 1985. In order to combat the irregular tactics employed by such men, the Soviets developed specialized tactics to protect the vehicles that mujahideen ambushes regularly targeted. One or more combat vehicles would take up positions on dominant terrain to provide covering fire for another vehicle or a group as they advanced. The group thus enabled to proceed would then halt on a dominant feature of its own, there to cover the forward movement of the previous covering group. Dismounted motor-rifle units usually deployed personnel with heavy machine guns in one or more monitoring positions to cover the advance of the rest of the unit. (© Reza/Webistan/Corbis)

Resistance fighters firing at aircraft. Initially the mujahideen relied on the Soviet-designed 12.7mm DShK (seen here) and 14.5mm KPV heavy machine guns, but in later years they received Chinese-made versions as well. Although heavily armoured Hind helicopters and fighter-bombers remained largely immune from such weapons, concentrated ground fire sometimes deterred pilots from patrolling in areas in which the resistance deployed large numbers of HMGs. (© Reuters/Corbis)

The defenders shot down two helicopters in the process, but Soviet fixed-wing air support hampered further mujahideen success and destroyed several of their positions, killing 18 men. Their commander, Jalaluddin Haqqani (1950–) and 150 of his men were trapped by debris blocking the cave in which they lay in wait, but by a quirk of fate the carpet bombing that followed cleared the entrance and facilitated their escape. With no answer to the air strikes, the defenders opted to move on to the offensive, thereby remaining close enough to the attackers to avoid fire from the aircraft. Haqqani managed to overrun four landing zones, taking several hundred prisoners in the process – a circumstance that led the Soviets later to alter their tactics to avoid setting down helicopters in the midst of resistance positions that could shower descending aircraft with RPG and machine gun fire. But the mujahideen could do no more: Soviet and Afghan forces managed to

outflank Haqqani's position, forcing his men to fall back, and as reinforcements continued to appear around Zhawar, the resistance declined to maintain what amounted to an impossible defence and scattered.

DRA troops held Zhawar for a few hours but unaccountably neglected either to carry off the arms and ammunition that remained for the taking, or even to destroy them. Likewise, they made a feeble attempt to destroy the caves with explosives, while their opponents, refusing to withdraw without registering a final act of defiance, fired rockets at regime forces as if to signify the hollow victory that Zhawar represented for Kabul. Indeed, within a few weeks the base returned to operational status, garrisoned once again by resistance fighters, whose losses in the defence of Zhawar amounted to 281 killed and 363 wounded, with government forces suffering similar losses. As hitherto commonly practised, though of course utterly forbidden by international law, the mujahideen executed all of the officers they captured and compelled the soldiers to submit to two years' manual labour in rear logistical areas, with the promise of release after serving their time. Zhawar demonstrated that the resistance could not, in fixed positions, hold out against the concentrated firepower of Soviet and DRA forces. Nevertheless, in turn, although outwardly successful, their opponents could not muster the numbers to hold positions seized in the operation.

The capture of the major resistance base at Zhawar in spring 1986 signified a welcome development for regime forces in an otherwise frustrating campaign against opponents who proved exceedingly difficult to pin into position, and who seldom entered an engagement except where the ground, weather, numbers or other factors played to their advantage. But successes such as Zhawar failed to conceal the fact that Soviet and DRA forces could rarely exert more than a temporary impact over a limited area before insufficient numbers and military priorities elsewhere obliged their withdrawal to their bases of operation. Thus, taking ground posed comparatively few problems for conventional forces enjoying vastly superior firepower; holding that ground, on the other hand, required a far greater commitment in manpower than the Soviets were prepared to make. Withdrawal inevitably left in its wake a vacuum that the mujahideen quickly filled.

In the south, the regime largely controlled Kandahar, but it could never hold down the region permanently against resistance units under such talented commanders as Haji Abdul Latif, or the numerous other smaller rebel factions formed and held together by tribal loyalties or clustered around a particularly charismatic leader. If fighting in southern Afghanistan, particularly in and around Kandahar, tended to manifest itself in skirmishing, in contrast to the larger-scale operations conducted in the east by Soviet troops, it nonetheless occupied the attention and energy of regime forces for years. The absence of set-piece battles, co-ordinated campaigns and great sweeps may suggest a sense of tranquillity, but nothing could be further from the case. Low-intensity warfare by definition does not yield heavy casualties in the short term (there is no Somme, El Alamein or Stalingrad), but gradual, mounting losses inflicted by the mujahideen slowly ground down Soviet morale, encouraging the cycle of atrocity and counter-atrocity so characteristic of irregular warfare. Indeed, both sides committed barbarities against each other until they became commonplace. The Soviets sometimes cold-bloodedly dispatched prisoners by dropping them from helicopters after interrogation, or simply shot them in the head. The resistance, for its part, sometimes tortured its captives by means of castration, disfigurement or skinning alive. A lingering death could be created by securing the prisoner to pegs planted in the ground, his death coming slowly under a baking sun, or more swiftly via beheading.

Vladislav Tamarov, a young Soviet conscript, observed some of the more common varieties of atrocity committed by both sides:

I saw houses burned by the Mujahadeen, as well as disfigured bodies of prisoners they'd taken. But I saw other things too: villages destroyed by our shelling and bodies of women, killed by mistake. When you shoot at every rustling in the bushes, there's no time to think about who's there. But for an Afghan, it didn't matter if his wife had been killed intentionally or accidentally. He went into the mountains to seek revenge (Tamarov 2005: 116).

Often the combatants simply refused to offer quarter, as Tamarov recalled in the case of one mujahid with his arms raised above his head in token of surrender.

According to the rules of war, I should have taken him prisoner. But there were no rules in this war. I had no choice – there were only three of us, and we didn't know how many of them were left. To this day, I remember the fear in his eyes; it was so strong, that it was hard for me to take aim. All I could do was close my eyes and pull the trigger. (Tamarov 2005: 126)

The Soviets, far from pursuing a 'hearts and minds' campaign in order to encourage the population's sympathies with the government in Kabul, committed atrocities with shocking regularity against villages suspected of aiding the resistance or in retaliation for ambushes. Such ruthless, counterproductive acts certainly forced out vast numbers of the inhabitants – denying the mujahideen some of the rural support so vital to their operations – but the short-term advantage thus gleaned by shifting populations and destroying farmland by sowing aerial mines or bombing paled in significance against the numbers of survivors thus driven into the hands of the guerrillas. Thousands joined local mujahideen groups, while most fled across the Pakistani border to join the resistance at its base in Peshawar before returning, trained, armed, bitter and vengeful. A young refugee Afghan boy of about eight graphically related an account of the Soviets arriving in his village:

Soviet block-and-destroy operation

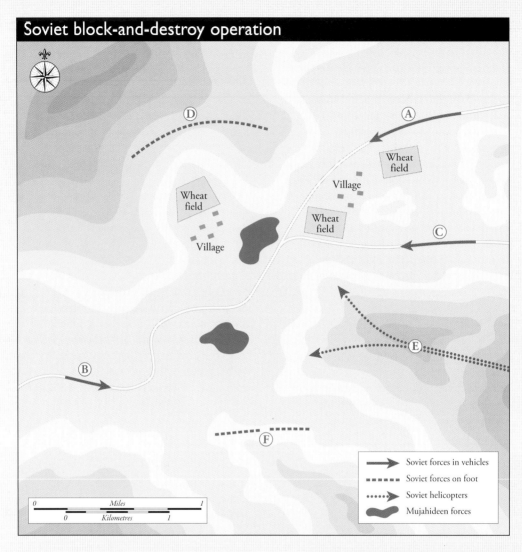

Soviet forces in vehicles
Soviet forces on foot
Soviet helicopters
Mujahideen forces

These operations involved dispatching forces to areas known to contain sizeable concentrations of mujahideen, blocking their retreat before engaging and destroying them; several independent mujahideen forces would sometimes gather in one place to plan and execute a major operation. In this case, Soviet ground troops operating out of tracked BMP-1 infantry fighting vehicles will comb through the villages, killing or driving out into the open any mujahideen forces taking refuge among the local population, while various other combat elements, including air assault forces inserted by helicopter, will press the enemy from various directions, denying escape routes wherever possible. It is very unlikely that the Soviet forces will take prisoners; quarter was seldom given.

To this end, three motorized rifle companies – (A), (B) and (C) – together totalling about 300 men, will converge on mujahideen positions from three directions by road. A mountain-rifle battalion (D), about 600 men strong, will arrive in BMP-1s, then advance across the heights towards a village below that is known to provide aid to the enemy.

Meanwhile, 12 Mi-24 Hind helicopter gunships (E) will approach to engage the enemy while they remain in open ground; they will arrive in two six-ship groups, both flying in a pattern-eight, one group behind the other. They will approach at low altitude, using flares to distract any infra-red missiles. At 7,500m from their target they will attack with rockets from an altitude of about 80m, but will remain beyond 1,500m so as to avoid enemy machine-gun fire.

To the south, poised on an eminence, lies an 90-man air assault company (F), inserted by air using Mi-8 Hip helicopters and carrying BM-12 rockets, 82mm mortars, AK-74s and RPK-74 light machine guns. Their mission is to deploy on heights overlooking a mujahideen position and prevent the escape of any enemy forces driven off by other elements of the Soviet offensive.

If properly co-ordinated, swift Soviet deployment by road and air, including the use of small numbers of tanks, BMPs or BTRs – with or without accompanying dismounted troops – stands to provide the Soviets with decisive results.

*The mujahideen went back to the mountains.
They [the Russians] came in our direction. We
were all in bed. They broke down the door and
came in. The door was smashed. We were all
frightened and jumped up. My brother didn't get
up but they forced him to stand up. They shot
my father and my brother. They lifted me up
and wounded me with their bayonets … I lay
down and cried. I was sad because my father
had been killed. My father was dead and was
lying on the ground. They took us outside. I saw
lots of people had been taken out of their houses
into the alleyways and killed. We went to the
bazaar. The shops, the shops had been burnt.
People had been killed. Everywhere women
had been killed, men had been killed, even
boys … They didn't leave a single one alive.
(Quoted in Gall 1988: 1)*

Appreciating at last that such
counterproductive methods only
galvanized the population's defiant
stance, and increasingly aware that their
military prospects were in decline, in the
summer of 1986 the Soviets eased their
campaign of driving civilians out of rural
areas in favour of seeking to secure their
co-operation with, if not allegiance to, the
regime in Kabul. This very belated, cynical
policy yielded few dividends from a people
marginalized by brutality and the forced
conscription of their menfolk into the
ranks of the DRA forces, as well as by the
presence of foreign troops supporting
a deeply unpopular regime. Thus, the
fighting merely continued as before.
On 6 July, the resistance conducted
a co-ordinated and successful attack
against an enormous Soviet convoy near
Maymaneh, the capital of Faryab province,

The Kunar Valley, the location of many Soviet sweeps
during the war. While the conflict affected all regions
of the country, especially that shown here, some
Afghans chose not to take sides. Many ordinary
peasants continued to harvest their crops and herd
their sheep, unconcerned about the politics of the war
so long as both sides did not interfere with their lives
and livelihoods. But when the war impinged, they often
fled their land and made for the mountains, or abroad
to Pakistan or Iran. (© Franco Pagetti/VII/Corbis)

Soviet soldier in Kabul in April 1988. Underfed and disillusioned troops sometimes exchanged Kalashnikovs, ammunition, rocket grenades and mortar shells for hashish. (© Patrick Robert/Sygma/Corbis)

near the Turkmenistan border, while in August the Soviets, supported by Afghan security forces, conducted substantial sweeps into the Lowghar Valley. On the 26th of the same month, the mujahideen set off massive explosions near Kabul when they fired 107mm and 122mm rockets into ammunition dumps at Kargha. Arriving to secure the area and the nearby town of Paghman, Afghan government forces met heavy opposition that left the area in ruins after fierce fighting. At about the same time, intense fighting took place in Herat.

During this third phase of the war the Soviets made more substantial use of special forces in the form of Spetsnaz and reconnaissance units, which sought to interdict the transfer of weapons, ammunition and supplies destined for the mujahideen from Pakistan. However, the frequency of contact during this particularly bloody period of the conflict

cost the Soviets 2,745 personnel killed, an average of 137 a month. These elite units performed well, and their deployment in greater numbers demonstrated the Soviets' eventual recognition that such forces could fulfil the pressing operational need for highly mobile, highly trained, specialist troops conversant with the tactics of counterinsurgency. But the Spetsnaz and other elite forces never accounted for more than 15 per cent of Soviet combat power and simply could not sustain the extremely punishing levels of continuous deployment imposed on them. Indeed, even as the number of special forces personnel reached its height in Afghanistan, 15,000 other troops withdrew in the summer of 1986, in line with Gorbachev's decision to bring home all field personnel by early 1989.

Phase Four: November 1986–February 1989

With the war clearly going badly and the Soviets now committed to withdrawing, they were keen to bolster the new president, Mohammad Najibullah Ahmadzai (1947–96), the brutish former head of the vicious KhAD. They were particularly enthusiastic about Najibullah's 'Policy of National Reconciliation', a plan to reconcile the government with moderate political and religious leaders of non-communist persuasion while simultaneously strengthening the numbers and capacity of Afghan forces and security personnel, in recognition of the somewhat disconcerting fact that the regime would soon depend largely upon its own wits and resources to defeat the insurgency after final Soviet withdrawal.

Soviet forces naturally continued to support the efforts of the DRA, but by now commanders sought to preserve the lives of men soon to be dispatched home. Part of this process included increasing attacks by air, with heavy bomber strikes originating from the Soviet Union against mujahideen positions around Faisabad, Jalalabad and

Kandahar, which ground troops had already evacuated. The Soviets also unsuccessfully launched raids against insurgent rocket batteries shelling Kabul on a regular basis, and, as their last forces were withdrawing, aircraft hit the Panjshir Valley in an effort to keep Massoud's forces distracted there. But in this fourth and final phase the Soviets largely occupied themselves with completing their withdrawal, which they carried out in two stages: between May and August 1988 and from November 1988 to February 1989.

Apart from Soviet troop withdrawals, this phase of the war is notable for two other features: the introduction into resistance arsenals of the Stinger ground-to-air missile, whose effectiveness, though often exaggerated, nevertheless manifested itself in the serious blow it inflicted on Soviet air power; and the increasing frequency of raids conducted by the mujahideen over the Soviet border.

With respect to the Stinger, Bocharov witnessed at first hand the weapon's lethality against helicopters:

Suddenly, the chopper shuddered, as though it had collided with something, pitched over to one side, and seemed to halt in midair. Then, describing an imperfect parabola, it seemed to head back for the ground. But it wasn't flying back – it was falling, falling like a stone. A [missile] had pierced its stabilizer, wrecked the metal, and set the fuselage on fire. The pilots made desperate efforts to pull out, but it was useless. The chopper, with its full load of wounded, roared toward the ground. (Bocharov 1990: 43)

Observers dispute the number of Soviet aircraft downed by the Stinger, but it may well have accounted for hundreds. At the very least it induced pilots to fly at higher altitudes, attracting to themselves the derisive appellation of 'cosmonaut' – a contemptuous reference to their staying out of range.

Although the mujahideen inflicted only small degrees of damage in cross-border raids into the Soviet Union's Central Asian republics, they palpably established the fact

Stinger surface-to-air missiles yielded their first kills when near Jalalabad in September 1986 the mujahideen downed three unsuspecting Mi-24 gunships in a matter of seconds, thus challenging the Soviets' complete supremacy in the air. Although the US purchased Soviet-designed weapons from abroad in order to mask American involvement in the war, the appearance of Stingers clearly revealed Washington's covert participation. These Taliban militiamen were photographed in the late 1990s with an ageing Stinger, dating from the Soviet war. (© Reuters/Corbis)

that not only had the Soviets failed to bring the insurgency under control, but also that the resistance could penetrate enemy territory almost at will, such as during an operation conducted about 20km (12½ miles) north of the Amu Darya River in April 1987, when insurgents bombarded a factory in Tajikistan with rockets.

As before, though, such small-scale operations functioned in tandem with much larger engagements, such as the renewed heavy fighting that took place in Herat on 7 April, when encounters in the streets resulted in over 50 casualties inflicted against Soviet and DRA personnel. The following month the Soviets launched

an operation specifically intended to relieve the besieged garrison of Ali Sher in Paktia province. Although a Soviet success, the mujahideen struck back to ensure their opponents did not establish a permanent presence in the area, forcing them out in mid-June. The following month, on 27 July, particular trouble erupted in the south (never

Left: Afghan government troops on armoured personal carriers, February 1989. As with many counterinsurgencies before and since, the Soviets and their Afghan allies could not deploy the requisite numbers and supplies to maintain permanent control over the areas that they cleared of resistance, often obliging them to repeat the same operation.
(© Patrick Robert/Sygma/Corbis)

a tranquil place, even before the Soviet invasion), when a mujahideen missile brought down a plane containing senior Soviet and Afghan officers while attempting a landing at the airport in Kandahar. At about the same time, the small Soviet garrison at Bamiyan abandoned the city after holding off a mujahideen attack. The resistance stepped up its campaign of terror in Kabul when on 9 October it planted a car bomb that killed 27 people, one of many urban terrorist attacks launched by the resistance in towns and cities across Afghanistan.

Further proof of the Soviets' inability to hold much more than the ground on which they stood became evident after the successful relief of the besieged city of Khost, in which 18,000 troops, of whom 10,000 were Soviets, succeeded in re-opening the road between Gardez and Khost to convoys between November and December 1987. The Soviets eventually abandoned these positions at the end of January 1988, in another striking example of their inability to secure even positions of significant strategic value while burdened by other pressing demands on troops and supplies. Shortly thereafter, as part of their policy of withdrawal, the Soviets left Kandahar to an uncertain future under tenuous DRA control.

With Soviet forces evacuating the south of the country, activity continued in other regions, where resistance fighters, emboldened by their opponents' withdrawal, struck in Kabul on 27 April 1988. A truck bomb exploded during the tenth anniversary of the communist takeover, killing six and

A BMP-1 or BMP-2 infantry fighting vehicle, armed with a 30mm cannon. The Soviets deployed such vehicles and tanks in Afghanistan, but these proved of very limited use in mountainous areas, while APCs posed problems of their own. The Soviet rifleman depended on his personnel carrier both for his own transport as well as for his equipment that the vehicle conveyed, with the specifications of his uniform and gear naturally reflecting this. The standard flak jacket, for instance, weighed 16kg (35lb), totally impractical for an assault conducted several kilometres away from his vehicle, since exhaustion soon put a halt to any effective advance.
(© Patrick Robert/Sygma/Corbis)

wounding several times more. Bombs planted in vehicles formed only a single aspect of the mujahideen's renewed attacks in Kabul. On 9 May they fired rockets into the city, killing at least 23 civilians, with many more similar attacks to follow over the coming months. Such acts of terror failed to weaken the regime's grip on the city, but they exposed in stark terms the futility of the authorities' efforts to protect the inhabitants from indiscriminate violence and thus to demonstrate a capacity to maintain security even within urban areas, much less within the seat of government itself. In short, by operating in and around Kabul seemingly at will, the mujahideen sought to underline the inevitability of the regime's downfall.

In May and June 1988, renewed fighting between local resistance forces and government troops took place in Kandahar, a city no longer garrisoned by Soviet troops, but with no decisive results. Still, the mujahideen succeeded on 17 June in seizing Qalat, the capital of Zabol province. As the first such city to fall to the resistance, Qalat was a place of symbolic importance. The victory proved short-lived, however. Straddling the main road between Kabul and Kandahar, Qalat enjoyed a level of strategic significance which the regime could not ignore lest its retention by the mujahideen signal the general defection of other towns and cities across the country. As such, DRA forces took particular pains to retake the city four days later.

All told, this last phase of the war cost the Soviets 2,262 fatalities, with an average of 87 deaths per month.

Conclusions

An analysis of the operational record of the conflict reveals that the Soviets completely failed to accept that their doctrine and training ill-suited them for the type of war into which they plunged themselves. Fully capable of undertaking operations on a grand scale and in a conventional context, apart from their

Mujahideen on a captured APC, possibly a BTR-152, BTR-60PBm or BTR-70. The assertion that the resistance benefited significantly from the production of narcotics is erroneous. Some groups farmed opium poppies in spite of the Soviet destruction of the irrigation systems common throughout Afghanistan and made modest profits, but only where melting snows made possible a substitute system of irrigation.
(© Pascal Manoukian/Sygma/Corbis)

special forces Soviet troops were not armed, equipped or trained for a platoon leaders' war, which entailed locating and destroying small, elusive, local forces which only stood their ground and fought when terrain and circumstances favoured them, and otherwise struck quickly before rapidly melting away. There were no fixed positions, no established front lines and rarely any substantial bases of operation for the insurgents. Whereas the Soviets could perform extremely well at the operational level, complete with large-scale all-arms troop movements, this could not be easily adapted to circumstances on the ground – where the war was a tactical one, in which Soviet tactics did not conform to the requirements of guerrilla warfare. Soviet equipment, weapons and doctrine suited their forces well for a confrontation on a massive scale on the northern European plain, a context in which they were confident in employing massed artillery to obliterate NATO's defensive positions before driving through the gaps created to crush further resistance and to pursue the remnants of shattered units.

Soviet tactics simply did not accord with their opponent's fighting methods. No benefit accrued by massing artillery to carry out a bombardment of an enemy who seldom concentrated in large numbers and who dispersed at will, reforming elsewhere for the next ambush or raid. Soviet conscripts and reservists could dismount from a personnel carrier and deploy rapidly for the purpose of laying down suppressive fire on an enemy unit or sub-unit of like composition, but the tactics and standard battle drills of the typical motorized rifle regiment failed to match the attacks of a highly mobile, fluid enemy who refused to fight on terms consistent with Soviet doctrine. Air assault and Spetsnaz forces learned to adapt their tactics to meet the demands of a guerrilla war, and in this regard they achieved some success. But the level of innovation required to defeat such a wide-scale insurgency proved beyond the means of Soviet forces as a whole, and thus must be seen as one amongst many factors that doomed them to ultimate failure.

The Soviets laboured under the illusion that because the heavy application of military force had succeeded in the past, it was bound also to succeed in current operations. Important precedents existed to support this view, including the numerous campaigns conducted against independence movements as long ago as the Russian Civil War and into the 1920s, when Bolshevik forces put down revolts in the Ukraine, Central Asia, the Transcaucasus and even the Far East. During World War II – quite apart from the Herculean efforts first to oust the Germans from home soil and then to drive on Berlin – Soviet forces quashed serious opposition from Ukrainian and Belorussian nationalists, some of whom carried on the struggle after 1945. After all this, and when their forces easily put down the risings in East Germany, Hungary and Czechoslovakia, Soviet forces could be forgiven for thinking that their might stood invincible against all foes, conventional and unconventional alike.

Afghanistan exploded this fallacy. Even when they adapted to new circumstances, the Soviets failed to deploy sufficient numbers of forces to fulfil their mission. They could not possibly hope to defeat the insurgency when spread across such a vast area. The defence of bases, airfields, cities and lines of communication alone committed the bulk of Soviet forces to static duties when circumstances demanded unremitting strike operations against the insurgents, thereby maintaining the initiative and obliging the resistance to look to their own survival in favour of attacks of their own. Soviet regiments, companies and platoons routinely stood under-strength, with regiments often down to single battalion strength and companies little more than oversized platoons. Much of this

Soviet troops waving from atop their armoured fighting vehicles as they leave Afghanistan. World opprobrium, dissent at home, the ill effects of drug-taking amongst Soviet troops, mounting casualties and the steady economic drain on the economy by a conflict that is estimated to have cost the Soviets $15 million per day all contributed to the Soviet leadership's decision to end the war in Afghanistan. (© Reuters/Corbis)

Soviet Army base in Kabul, May 1988. Once the Soviets realized that their mere presence could not defeat the insurgency, in the time-honoured tradition of counterinsurgency they accompanied that force with a programme of reforms meant to modernize Afghan agriculture and bureaucracy while seeking to draw on the aid of collaborators. Such measures failed miserably amidst a traumatised and ungrateful population. (© Patrick Robert/Sygma/Corbis)

occurred despite the large bi-annual troop levies, which certainly furnished the men required, but whose numbers needlessly dwindled enormously due to poor field sanitation practices and inadequate diet, both of which contributed to the widespread dissemination of disease throughout the armed forces. A staggering one-quarter to one-third of a typical unit's strength was diminished by amoebic dysentery, meningitis, typhus, hepatitis and malaria, leaving actual field strength woefully low and so operationally compromised that commanders deemed it necessary to create composite units on an *ad hoc* basis.

In assessing the tactics and the fighting capacity of the 40th Army, one is struck by the generally poor performance of its regular units. As discussed earlier, they were trained to fight NATO forces on the plains of central Europe, with a strict adherence to orthodox formations and methods of attack. This obliged Soviet infantry to remain close to their armoured vehicles as they advanced down valleys in which the mujahideen took full advantage of the ground, much of it familiar to them. Performance improved amongst Soviet units as they examined their mistakes, but the problem of understrength units regularly dogged their efforts. Little could be done to counter the continuous drain on their morale caused by the anxiety imposed by the continuous threat of attack by guerrillas who sought out the Soviets' vulnerabilities by day, but especially by night, so wearing down morale and causing physical and mental exhaustion. The war required immense physical efforts to make contact with an elusive opponent, but many Soviet soldiers lacked the stamina to cross the great distances necessary to come to grips with their enemy, not least across inhospitable terrain. Their training and equipment proved inadequate, and security and intelligence, particularly at the tactical level, proved poor to the extent that even when attempting to surround groups of insurgents, Soviet troops often failed to close the ring, thus allowing the enemy to escape through gaps or otherwise fight their way out. Overly confident in its fighting capacity, an attitude perhaps reinforced by a reputation of military invincibility earned as a consequence of the Red Army's extraordinary performance in World War II, and with no combat experience acquired since that time, the 40th Army found itself the victim of breathtaking hubris. Ill-trained for the type of warfare in which it engaged and incapable of achieving the unrealistic aims set for it by Moscow, it launched into the fray regardless.

Vladislav Tamarov, 103rd (Soviet) Guards Air Assault Division

A typical Russian conscript sent on active service to Afghanistan, Private Vladislav Tamarov served, according to his meticulously kept personal log, 621 days in theatre between 1984 and 1986. During this period he spent fully a third of that time on actual combat missions, many of these in the mountains where at the end of each day he gratefully acknowledged its passing with the stroke of a pen through the date. A 19-year-old draftee from Leningrad, in the course of a single minute's inspection Tamarov not only found himself inducted into the Soviet Army by visiting selection officers at the distribution centre to which he had been summoned, but two hours later seated on a plane bound for a training base in Uzbekistan, one of the Soviet Union's Central Asian republics. 'I wasn't scared. I wasn't surprised', he recalled. 'At that point I didn't care anymore because I understood that it was impossible to change anything' (Tamarov 2005: 1). He was right: young men from privileged families could usually pay their way out of military service, but that was not an option open to Tamarov. He remembered sceptically the reason a newspaper had furnished to justify Soviet intervention a few years before: 'At the request of the Afghan people, in order to bring comradely help to our Great Neighbor, Soviet troops entered Afghanistan' (Tamarov 2005: 112).

Tamarov knew nothing about Afghanistan apart from what he had learned on state television: propaganda reporting Soviet troops cheerfully performing public works for Afghan people whose lives they and the enlightened, communist government in Kabul bettered by planting trees and constructing schools and hospitals. Naturally such broadcasts said nothing about the number of Tamarov's fellow citizens who had died fighting the mujahideen, but he did know that the bodies repatriated from Afghanistan and filling the cemeteries at home lay in graves marked with black stones bearing no details beyond the young occupants' names – the dates and other inscriptions suspiciously absent – so as not to associate them with the mounting rate of fatalities sustained in an unpopular war. The whole unconscionable process had begun even before the dead had arrived back on Soviet soil, when the authorities

A Soviet air assault paratrooper. The most successful Soviet ground forces tended to be their air assault forces, as they were better equipped, trained and motivated in the task of engaging with the mujahideen at close quarters. But they were never available in sufficient numbers, with units routinely under-strength. Ideally, air assault forces ought to have occupied elevated terrain along convoy routes, but this was infrequently practised and such troops found themselves severely over-stretched. (© Patrick Robert/Sygma/Corbis)

sent a curt, impersonal notification to the parents of those killed in action stating simply: 'Your son perished while fulfilling his international duty in Afghanistan.'

Officers provided slightly more in the way of explanation for the war to Tamarov and his fellow recruits during their training, claiming they were 'defending the southern borders of the Soviet Union, as well as the Afghan revolution', but such a vague justification probably meant little to any but those who volunteered to serve. Tamarov himself was supposed to receive six months' training at boot camp, but the army reduced this to just three, during the course of which he made three parachute jumps in order to qualify for admission to the air assault unit he wished to join. On completion, military authorities sent him to Kabul, where Tamarov's surprise at finding reddish-coloured mountains instead of skyscrapers betrayed his utter ignorance of the country to which he had been sent in defence of its communist government. Headquartered in the Bala Hissar fortress on the outskirts of Kabul, Tamarov was perplexed to discover himself, notwithstanding all his specialized training, assigned to mine-sweeper training on his first day.

Ten days later his new education began. He sometimes rode on a mine trawler – a tank without its turret – or aboard an armoured personnel carrier with other minesweepers, at the front of a convoy. When the column reached an area suspected of mines, it halted so Tamarov and his colleagues could jump down to investigate. Mine-detection proved slow, nerve-racking and painstaking, requiring Tamarov to employ metal detectors and listening devices and to drive probes into the ground, feeling for a solid object and the slightly hollow, tell-tale sound that distinguished a rock from an explosive device. A missed or misinterpreted sound could cost him his life. He regularly checked roads and paths, particularly in the mountains, disarming or blowing up ordnance he discovered and laying anti-personnel shrapnel mines to defend his group while it camped for the night.

Sometimes he simply created an *ad hoc* explosive device by linking two grenades together with a wire, which he then had to disarm in the morning.

Having lived his life entirely in Leningrad, Tamarov found Afghanistan exotic:

… enormous skies – uncommonly starry – occasionally punctuated by the blazing lines of tracers. And spread out before you, this mysterious Asian capital where strange people were bustling about like ants in an anthill: bearded men, faces darkened by the sun, in solid-colored wide cotton trousers and long shirts. Their modern jackets, worn over those outfits, looked completely unnatural. And women, hidden under plain dull garments that covered them from head to toe; only their hands visible, holding bulging shopping bags, and their feet, in worn-out shoes or sneakers, sticking out from under the hems. (Tamarov 2005: 114)

Ignorant of the true reasons for Soviet intervention in a strange, far-off place, and motivated by nothing more than survival, Tamarov unwittingly symbolized a typical cog in the vast Soviet political machine in which the conscript fought out of no higher motivation than that of simple self-preservation. Therein lay disturbingly familiar echoes of Vietnam:

Now I'm often asked if I thought the war was a just war when I was there. How can I answer? I was a boy who was born and raised in quiet, beautiful Leningrad, a boy who loved his parents and went obediently to school. A boy who was yanked out of that life and dumped in a strange land where there was a real war going on, where life followed different rules. And the most important rule was simple: only those who kill first will survive. There, we didn't have 'smart thoughts.' We shot at those who were shooting at us; we killed those who were killing us. (Tamarov 2005: 2)

Thus, lacking any motivation associated with fighting for a higher cause, much less the attainment of some concrete good, Tamarov unknowingly succeeded in identifying in a few words the vast chasm which separated the perspective of the typical Soviet conscript from that of his counterpart in the resistance. Whilst the former counted down the days until his release from service – in the meantime clinging desperately to the hope of survival in a hostile land – the latter, the simple mujahid, actively looked for a fight as a natural warrior accustomed to hardship and sacrifice and bred in the defence of his religion.

For the first 18 months of service in Afghanistan Tamarov did not think about the hardships he suffered or the possibility of death. Being shot at became a curiosity and the risks merely commonplace:

It's probably simply that we lived alongside death all the time. And when you live next to death like that, you don't think about it anymore, you just try to encounter it as seldom as possible. I remember when we were ambushed once, I had to jump out from behind a rock and run about thirty-five meters under a hail of bullets. In those moments I didn't think about death – it was just so hard to tear my back away from the cliffs and go. But when there were only six months left for me to serve, then I knew the meaning of fear. You can hear that it's not your bullet, but still you press close to the ground and you're terrified, not just of dying, but it's terrifying to think of dying when you're so close to home. (Tamarov 2005: 4)

He spent much of his time searching for *dushman* (bandit) positions in the mountains, into which helicopters regularly inserted his unit. As for the French in Algeria in the 1950s and the Americans in Vietnam in the '60s, the helicopter became an indispensable component of counterinsurgency operations in Afghanistan, and by safely conveying troops over the hazards posed by mines and roadside ambushes – not to mention sparing them the sheer leg-work of traversing elevated and broken ground – proved a much-preferred alternative to the standard means of transport.

When we went by convoy, there were always lots of problems: checking the road [for mines], and

Afghan mujahid in Kunar province, 1980. As guerrillas, the resistance naturally did not organize itself into formal military units, thus rendering any even vaguely accurate tabulation of their strength extremely speculative. Estimates suggest between 90,000 and 300,000 men operated in the field at any given time. (© Pascal Manoukian/Sygma/Corbis)

the dust and wind. The trip was always long and uncomfortable, and they unloaded us far from where we were supposed to end up. Sometimes we had to spend a couple of days climbing mountains just to get into the right quadrant. Getting back to the base by convoy was even worse. (Tamarov 2005: 28)

As a member of an elite unit, Tamarov regularly took part in the ambushes that specially trained Soviet formations like his conducted with admirable proficiency against the resistance – in effect, 'fighting fire with fire'. But whereas the cover of darkness normally concealed the attacker's position while he lay in wait, Tamarov sometimes disconcertingly found himself and his comrades exposed in an unexpected fashion:

… We'd been going for several hours. A bright white moon lit up the valley with merciless light; we kept having to hide in the long shadows cast

Soviet soldier observing the unloading of food in Kabul in February 1989. Most of their infantry consisted of motor-rifle formations whose personnel rode in armoured personnel carriers, from which they operated within a distance not meant to exceed 200m. Their equipment, weaponry and uniform were designed with this in mind. These tactics suited the kind of fighting anticipated in northern Europe, whereas service in Afghanistan required light infantry, of which the Soviets deployed none but small numbers of special forces. (© Sam Sherbell/Corbis Saba)

A mujahid. Young men like this demonstrated that well-motivated, ideologically driven insurgents, adequately supplied from abroad and employing tactics suited to the circumstances, could overcome a much better-armed opponent. (© Pascal Manoukian/Sygma/Corbis)

by the mountains. And the longer we walked, the higher the moon rose, [and] the shorter the shadows became. In an hour, we'd have no place left to hide. In that cold light, we were easy targets. I never knew that night could be brighter than day. I wanted to fall down, hide, and wait for the sun to rise. (Tamarov 2005: 30)

Tamarov did not record in his brief reminiscences whether the stunning Afghan landscape somehow compensated for the rigours of campaigning, but he did admire Afghanistan for its beauty, particularly the Panjshir Valley, northeast of Kabul – albeit never a place for relaxing lest a sniper's bullet strike him whilst he sunned himself on a rocky perch. There, only a dreary guard post (*zastava*) with a handful of other soldiers offered a modicum of real protection. Some held only a dozen men or so, with these often serving in cramped conditions for as much as 18 months without relief, the men suffering from boredom, monotony, bad quality food and water, and virtually no entertainment besides the occasional television. Worst of all, living in such confined and unsanitary conditions the miserable inhabitants easily spread disease amongst one another and suffered psychologically and physically from the constant threat of insurgent attack. Such posts might sit perched upon inaccessible points, such as atop heights overlooking Afghan villages or routes of supply, so remote in fact as to be incapable of resupply except by helicopter. *Zastavas* regularly came under attack, though none ever fell to the mujahideen owing to the strength of their structures, not to mention the strenuous efforts made by their diminutive garrisons and their total reliance on the staggering firepower of their heavy machine guns.

Still, appreciating the precarious nature of their existence, the natural instinct for survival prevalent amongst the isolated detachments often induced them to make themselves tolerable to the local population in a sort of 'live-and-let-live' policy. This was unofficially applied all over Afghanistan by small groups of otherwise natural antagonists simply trying to carry on life as tolerably as possible in the midst of a war in which neither party wished to participate. This fact alone shatters the mythology underpinning the popularly held yet simplistic view that every Afghan peasant supported the mujahideen, and that every Soviet soldier committed senseless acts of brutality, thus rendering himself utterly abhorrent to the inhabitants. There is some truth in both assertions, but the reality – as in all generalizations about war – lies somewhere in between.

Paradoxically, when Tamarov finally did return to Leningrad – now as a veteran or *afganets* (plural *afgantsy*) – although he was painfully anxious to resume a normal home life, he felt a powerful urge to return to active service in Afghanistan. 'I wanted to bang against the walls, drop everything, and go back. Go back there, where I knew my purpose, where I knew the value of life,

where I was needed' (Tamarov 2005: 4). This is not surprising, since the experience, as for so many soldiers through the ages, gave a meaning so patently absent from life as previously lived; but above all it formed a bond between him and his comrades. 'Unfortunately, there were cowards there, and there were a few creeps there. And that's why the other kinds of guys, the ones I could go through fire and water with, that's why they are so dear to me' (Tamarov 2005: 6). Condemning the war as a meaningless failure, Tamarov identified the one redeeming aspect to be salvaged from an otherwise empty experience: looking out for his friends, the one feature that binds together all soldiers, regardless of context, during periods of armed conflict.

So the war was doomed, so it was pointless. Still, we soldiers in this war did what we could, as best we could. We gave our lives not for the sake of somebody's illusory goals, not for the sake of distorted ideals, but for the sake of those who were standing behind us. For the sake of those who ate from the same mess-tin. For the sake of those who, without hesitation, would do the same for us. (Tamarov 2005: 106)

Vladislav Tamarov may well have suffered from post-traumatic stress disorder, for within two years of returning from Afghanistan he got married, then divorced, entered and subsequently dropped out of college, and worked as a labourer, a performer and finally a street sweeper – one of countless veterans who struggled to find his way after the trauma of service in a war in which he never believed.

A glimpse of rural Afghanistan

Afghanistan has a turbulent, often violent, history. It is a land of hardened, brave, highly independent peoples who have adapted to a harsh and unforgiving climate and maintain a fierce sense of independence, an unshakable religious faith and a deep sense of loyalty to family and clan. Many of these features stem from the country's long association not merely with inter-tribal strife – certainly an historically prominent and pervasive feature of Afghan life in its own right – but with foreign intervention and war, pre-dating even Alexander the Great's incursion in the 4th century BC. Since this time every successive invader, whether Persian, Mongol, Briton, or one of many others besides, has encountered intractable resistance and often military disaster. In light of all this, perhaps unsurprisingly, the Afghan character, if often generalized and stereotyped, has followed a familiar pattern stretching across the centuries – particularly its martial qualities, as one Western observer noted during the height of the Soviet occupation:

Afghans are a tough people who can live on bread and goat's milk, and most who have known them have commented on their extraordinary personal dignity and love of freedom. The Afghans believe that the greatest of all virtues are revenge and hospitality. They never forgive an injury, yet paradoxically they do not turn away a guest even if he is a tribal or personal foe. These qualities are particularly associated with the Pushtuns. The romantic Image Is of a tall, bearded tribesman striding along a rocky path with a rifle on his shoulder and a fierce glint in his eyes. His land is everything and his home, with its thick mud walls, stout gates, and watch towers at the corners, is his castle. His prestige and honor depend on his ability to defend them against a foreign invader, against another

valley – or against another branch of his family. It sounds gloriously heroic, but from the cold view of politics it amounts to ordered anarchy. (Bonner 1987: 25–26)

The literal meaning of 'Afghanistan' is simply 'Land of the Afghans', a term which deceptively suggests that its people compose a single ethnic group, a circumstance which could not be further from reality. In fact, Afghanistan, situated in the heart of Central Asia, stands within a crossroads of major geographical and cultural regions, with Iran immediately to its west and the Indian sub-continent to its east, with Pakistan sharing a lengthy border both to its east and south, thus rendering Afghanistan land-locked. Even the Far East is not too distant, for the Pamir Mountains extend like a finger far into China's Sinkiang province. In this very brief sketch, space precludes discussion of the country's varying topography and climate, but one may soon acquire an impression of its impressive size via simple comparison. Afghanistan is about 395,000km^2 (245,000 square miles), or roughly the size of France or the state of Texas, with extremely varying terrain. It is dominated by mountains and deserts, relatively few major rivers and numerous narrow mountain valleys. The country consists of harsh, inhospitable terrain that renders living hard, demanding considerable labour on the land in order to eke out a living.

Indeed, when the war began only about 12 per cent of the land was under cultivation annually, owing to shortages of water. Land is irrigated where possible, but dry farmed land produces wheat and barley, although never in great abundance. While pre-war Afghanistan certainly ranked high amongst the poorest countries of the world, its people did not suffer from acute hunger, for its soil, though hardly rich, sustains a variety of basic foodstuffs including corn, rice, sugar beets, sugar cane, oilseed, vegetables, nuts and fruit, all supplemented with meat in the form of lamb, beef and chicken. Farmers graze principally sheep and goats, and employ water buffalo as plough animals, or the yak in the Pamir Mountains. Of a pre-war population of about 14 million – although this figure is disputed, with up to 18 million claimed – 85 per cent of Afghans worked the land or served in agriculturally related professions, enabling this relatively small population to survive with such a diminutive area of cultivated land at its disposal. Having said this, the shortage of arable land was naturally worsened by the mines sown by the Soviets and the severe destruction wrought on the country's centuries-old irrigation systems.

Afghanistan is a land rich in horses, with hardy pack horses capable of carrying loads of up to 200lb (90kg) at about 3½mph (5½km/h), while donkeys perform almost as well, conveying about 150lb (68kg) at 2½mph (4km/h). Villagers often transport heavy loads on donkeys to town bazaars, selling what they can and returning bareback if possible. Mules are also used as pack animals, together with camels, the latter irritable and bad-tempered beasts having long since appeared in Afghanistan thanks to Central Asian nomads, who favoured the one-humped dromedary. Whatever their variety, camels in Afghanistan can carry loads of 400lb (180kg) in the plains and 300lb (135kg) in the mountains.

Introduced into the country in the mid-7th century, Islam – overwhelmingly of the Sunni faith – plays a fundamental part in daily life and politics and, in the absence of a proper national identity, supplies the only single unifying factor throughout the country. An American journalist visiting Afghanistan in 1985 observed part of the daily religious routine:

With the distant sound of a priest intoning the call to prayer and the crowing of cocks, the room came to life. The men … performed their morning ablutions, washing their faces, ears, arms, feet, legs, and genitals. Only then did they say their morning prayer, the first of the five that a Muslim must say every day. It was still early. The first prayer comes just before dawn. Some of the men went back to sleep. Others sat next to the lamps, which had been relit, and silently read from the Koran. Some of their copies were only palm-sized, to be carried in a man's pocket near his heart. Others were the size of a paperback book. (Bonner 1987: 7)

Apart from the Muslim faith, the dominant characteristics of the Afghan people are their ethnic diversity, overwhelmingly rural pattern of life and dearth of education. When the war began illiteracy ran at 90–95 per cent, since as a basically agrarian economy, the ability to read and write offered little advantage to village-dwellers, who in any event seldom had access to schooling. In terms of ethnicity, the Pushtuns form the largest group, representing at least 40 per cent of the population. Second are the Tajiks, making up approximately 20 per cent. The next three largest ethnic groups are all about the same proportion, being the Hazaras, the Uzbeks and the Aimaq. Yet in this multi-faceted society there are many other groups, including Turkmens, Kazaks, Wakhis, Baluchis, Qizilbash, Nuristanis and Kyrgyz, plus small minorities of Hindus, Sikhs and Jews. In all, Afghanistan is composed of at least 20 ethnic groups. Before and during the war these groups largely inhabited their own villages that surrounded towns of more mixed ethnicity, but in general ethnic integration in the countryside was rare. In the decades since Soviet occupation these trends have remained largely unchanged.

As the largest ethnic group in the country, the Pushtuns numbered about 6.5 million people when the war began. As a people, the Pushtuns are divided into two separate confederations of tribes, the Abdali or Durrani tribes, which live in the area around Kandahar and Herat, in the south and west respectively, and the Ghilzai, who live in the Nangarhar–Paktia region. The Ghilzai, along with the eastern tribes living in Pakistan who

Ethno-linguistic groups in and around Afghanistan

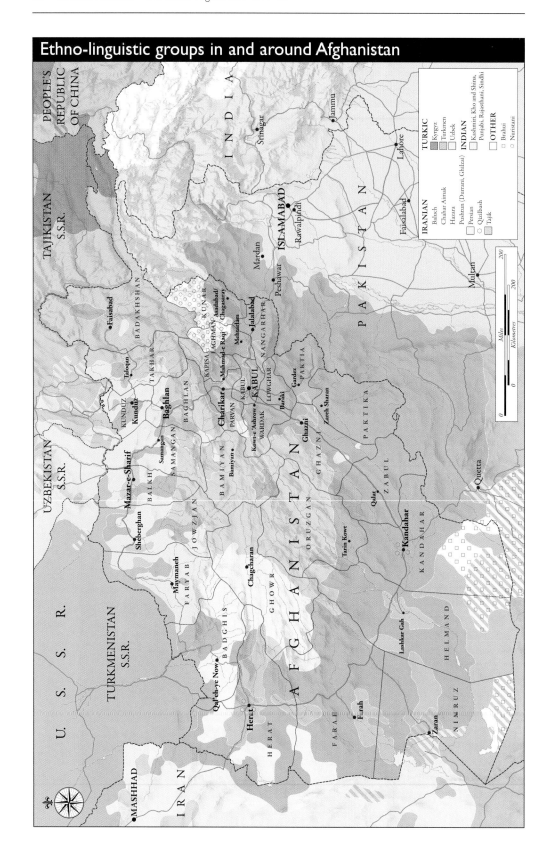

speak a different dialect, remain Pushtuns.
Thus when the British established the
modern boundary of Afghanistan and
India along the Durand Line in 1893,
they artificially separated ethnic Afghans
on both sides of the frontier. The Durranis
have provided the kings and oligarchy of
the country since the mid-18th century,
although during the communist era
(1973–92) national leaders were always
drawn from the Ghilzai confederacy.

The language spoken by Pushtuns is
related to Persian (Farsi), consists of a
complex system of grammar, with much
borrowing from Arabic and Persian, and
is written in an alphabet modified from
Arabic. Many Pushtuns learn Dari as well,
although Pushtu has formed the national
language since 1964. Nearly all Pushtuns are
Sunni Muslims, with a small number of Shi'a
among the eastern tribes. Tribal or inter-clan
interaction is based on a tribal legal system
known as Pushtunwali and much tribal
business is achieved through the tribal
assembly or *Jirga*.

Tajiks, who live in the northern,
northeastern and western parts of
Afghanistan, tend to speak Dari or Afghan
Persian, languages familiar to the Farsiwan
who are nevertheless unrelated ethnically,
as are the Qizilbash and the Hazara of the
central region of the country. All are related
linguistically, though the Tajiks and Farsiwan
are Sunni Muslims like most Pushtuns,
whereas the Qizilbash and the Hazara
profess Shi'a Islam in the style of the
Iranians. The Tajiks' loyalty rests with
village and family, but unlike the Pushtuns,
who place strong emphasis on genealogy
and tribal history, they can integrate
more successfully amongst their own
communities transplanted elsewhere in
the country. Historically they have been
denied positions of leadership in politics
or the military.

The Hazaras, who live in the central
part of Afghanistan, constitute less than
10 per cent of the population, and operate a
social structure in which various individuals
exercise significant authority, such as the

A typical Afghan village in Parvan province. If the
Soviets rained down destruction from the air on
such compounds, they also laid waste from the ground,
driving off the inhabitants, some of whom fled across
the borders to join the resistance at its base in Peshawar
before returning, trained, armed and extremely bitter.
(© Peter Langer/Peter Langer – Associated Media/
Design Pics/Corbis)

headman, chief, or *malik* (known locally
as a *mir*). His position of reverence derives
from his status as a landowner and from
a hereditary status purportedly descending
from the line of the Prophet Muhammad.
They are racially akin to the Mongols,
whose physical features set them readily
apart from other ethnic groups and have
led to discrimination over the centuries,
particularly by the Pushtuns, who often
used them as servants and slaves. The
Hazaras' adherence to the Shi'a sect has
furthered the degree of discrimination
directed against them, leaving them
somewhat on the fringes of society, a
condition exacerbated by their physical
isolation in the Hazarajat, which suffered
considerably less from Soviet occupation and
the Afghan civil war than most other areas.

Afghanistan also contains ethnic
Turkic-speaking groups living in the
north, including about a million Uzbeks,
200,000 Turkmens and about 15,000 Kazaks,
with co-ethnic peoples who at the time of the

war lived just over the border in Soviet Central Asia, and of course continue to do so in the now-independent republics. Most engage in agriculture or raise animals and speak their own language, although many are bilingual in Dari, which serves as the inter-ethnic language in the north. Generally speaking, the Uzbeks largely do not have strong tribal affiliations, whereas the Turkmens are closely tied to their own. Other ethnic groups, which make up the dozen or more smaller ethnicities in Afghanistan, speak between them more than 20 languages and dialects, though they are largely illiterate, and live almost entirely rural and for the most part segregated lives owing to geographical isolation.

Although the vast majority of Afghans live in the countryside, their patterns of life vary. Again, in addition to the binding nature of Islam, major unifying elements include close family relationships, patterns of living which stretch back dozens of generations, living close to and depending upon the land for practically all their needs, and a close observance to a faith in a largely unchanging life for the community as a whole. The typical Afghan adheres to a tradition of loyalty first to family, then to village, then to tribe and finally to ethnic group. This accounts for the poor development of patriotism, the long-standing problem of creating a national identity, and the difficulties associated with central government trying to spread its authority across a sprawling, mountainous conglomeration of diverse peoples speaking different languages and practising different customs. But if loyalty may be identified as a central guiding tenet of rural Afghan life, so too must bravery. In 1985 Arthur Bonner succinctly observed that:

Bravery is central to the Afghans. Being brave, or just seeming brave, shapes their attitudes toward life and the people around them. A large part of bravery in Afghan eyes is being able to bear pain and suffering. Honor is also important, and honor to the Afghans means not taking second place to anyone. They don't like to be pushed around. It offends their honor and makes them

want to get even. Revenge is another part of what it means to be a man in Afghanistan. The proof of these generalities is that Afghanistan, a poor and mountainous nation, with no technology and only light arms has literally stopped the Soviet Army dead in its tracks. (Bonner 1987: 1)

Accommodation in rural areas varies according to region, but before outlining its features it is germane to note that nationwide, one in nine houses in the countryside was believed uninhabitable in 1993, while in Nangarhar province, in the east, only 60 per cent were habitable. Of the approximately 15,000 villages in Afghanistan at the outset of the war, approximately 13 per cent of those in the southeast would suffer from problems of mines in agricultural areas, irrigation systems, near houses and along roads. Still, while wide-scale Soviet bombing depleted the countryside of its population, it did not fundamentally alter the basic structure of life for those who remained. Rural Pushtuns live in *qalas*, which are fortified, fired or sun-dried brick dwellings housing whole extended families and covered with curved roofs topped with flat ones. These structures feature rooms facing inwards towards a courtyard, with the rooms to the rear abutting the compound wall that can rise to 10ft or higher. The whole family lives within the safety of this compound, through whose single entrance all pass until the gate is bolted at night. While nuclear families occupy rooms exclusive to themselves, sleeping and keeping their personal possessions, the kitchen and toilet areas, as well as food storage areas and accommodation for guests, are shared by the extended family. Rural life depends heavily upon well-defined, gender-specific roles, with men responsible for building and maintaining accommodation, buying and selling goods and services, managing flocks of sheep and goats, and planting, ploughing, maintaining the irrigation system and any other work which demands their presence in public. Women care for children, assist in harvesting the crops, pursue crafts like quilt-making, and manage the family's domestic animals.

Most roles are also defined by the age of the individual, as more advanced age necessarily commands respect. In such a cohesive, traditional community as a large *qala*, one may find many dozens of people of several generations living and working together.

A group of *qalas* typically figure within or near a village, with irrigated fields either amidst them or nearby. Services, including shops, roads and public buildings in the vicinity, are basic. Many *qalas* contain a small mosque and sometimes a bathhouse within the compound, while others, such as those near the cities of Kandahar and Herat, often consist of more substantial structures of vaulted one-storey buildings constructed from sun-dried bricks. A group of such structures is sometimes found connected, with a single compound wall protecting everyone, which may include up to three generations of a family. Compounds normally contain a small stable for chickens and cows or other domestic animals, while storage areas hold supplies of food and fuel for a whole year. A well within the compound provides clean water, but rural-dwellers sometimes make use of streams or the irrigation system. To keep warm in the winter, rural Afghans burn charcoal in small braziers, which form a central point around which people sit, propping themselves up against the walls with cushions and bedding behind and a quilt covering the lower body. Sometimes in the centre of the room a brazier sits in a shallow depression dug into the ground, with a low table above covered by a quilt and tablecloth, so placed to function as a place for eating and socializing.

Rural Afghans tend to dress in a manner specifically intended to identify their ethnic group. Men often wear distinctive turbans or turban caps, with the method of tying the cloth (*lungi* or *dastar*) of the former identifying the group to which a man belongs. The turban cap (*kolah*) reflects a particular ethnic group by its specific embroidery. Most men also wear a loose-fitting, long-tailed cotton shirt that slips over the head and hangs to the knees or even lower, fastened by buttons on one

An elderly Afghan. Rural Afghan society and culture rests on the foundation of Pushtunwali, a widely practised code of conduct governing honour, hospitality and hostility. It demands defence of a person who takes refuge in one's house, vengeance against those who have killed a member of one's family, the punishment of adulterers, and exceptional hospitality to guests, even when complete strangers. (© Robert Maass/Corbis)

shoulder. Baggy trousers with a drawstring waist, out of which the shirt-tail usually remains untucked, together with a sleeveless, often distinctively embroidered waistcoat (*waskat*) or vest over the shirt, nearly completes this fairly standard outfit worn throughout the countryside. But notwithstanding variation according to region, one garment finds universal use, as Bonner noted in 1985:

A thin blanket is an integral part of the Afghan costume and has many uses. Generally a man folds it during the day and carries it on one shoulder. When the air is chilly, he wraps the blanket around his shoulders. If it is extra cold, he drapes it over his head to keep his ears warm. Under a hot sun he folds it into a thick pad and places it on top of his head to keep it cool. He spreads it on the ground as a clean area for prayers. He drapes it over his back like a curtain when he goes into an open field to relieve

A village in the Hindu Kush. Heavily agricultural and with a rurally based population, Afghanistan is especially noteworthy for the long tradition of tribal, ethnic and religious blood feuds that divide the country. There is little relief from these feuds except when foreign invasion temporarily unites a population that historically reverts back to inter-tribal conflict once the common enemy withdraws. (© Franco Pagetti/VII/Corbis)

himself. If a man has a number of things to carry, he wraps them in the blanket and knots the ends in front of his chest so that it becomes a sort of pack. If he sits on the ground he folds the blanket under him as a cushion and also to keep his trousers from getting dirty. But its main use is to keep him warm. (Bonner 1987: 14)

Women universally wear the shawl (or *chadar*), which is multi-functional, protecting her from dirt while allowing her to preserve a degree of modesty, since she can partly cover her face from a passing stranger by gripping a corner with her teeth. She can also wrap a baby and feed it in privacy by using one

end of her *chadar*, and by tying a corner of it she may transport small items. Rural women usually wear a white or coloured cotton shirt, baggy trousers, or an ankle-length skirt, with styles varying greatly according to region and climate. Footwear varies greatly, too, from open-toed and open-heeled leather or straw sandals to various types of boots, particularly in the colder north, where knitted, knee-length, thick wool stockings are worn inside boots during winter.

Numerous books devote themselves to Afghan history, geography, culture and religion, and nothing more than a thumbnail sketch of rural life may be outlined here. However, in delving further into these subjects the profound obstacles to change encountered by those politicians, bureaucrats and reformers who between 1978 and 1992 sought to tamper with the fundamentally traditional, religiously conservative nature of rural Afghanistan emerge in stark relief.

Arthur Bonner, *New York Times* journalist

Arthur Bonner began his time in journalism during World War II as a copyboy for a New York newspaper. He later worked as a radio news writer and television documentary producer with assignments in India, Africa and Latin America. He joined the National Broadcasting Company as a television producer, and although he officially retired in January 1985, his desire to write on the Soviet–Afghan War as a freelance journalist for *The New York Times* drew him to Afghanistan between February and October 1985.

In order to cross the porous border between Afghanistan and Pakistan's Northwest Frontier Province, Bonner required a sponsor – one of the seven Afghan resistance parties established in and around Peshawar who regularly sent fighters and aid across the border.

One furnished him with a guide and interpreter and directed him to a resistance safe house, which he discovered brimming with weapons and ammunition, including a Russian-made heavy machine gun of World War II vintage. These at least post-dated the numerous World War I bolt-action Enfield rifles that many mujahideen received covertly from Pakistani military stores managed by the ISI, Pakistan's equivalent to the CIA,

Afghan child refugees at study in a camp in Peshawar, Pakistan, in March 1983. Thousands of Afghans received radical religious instruction in makeshift schools established throughout Pakistan, making them a prime source of recruits for the mujahideen but also laying the foundation for the sort of Islamic militancy most often found in Saudi-financed *madrassas*. (© Alain Keler/Sygma/Corbis)

Men at prayer. Overwhelmingly Muslim, Afghanistan nonetheless reflects Islam in its many forms, including Hanafi Sunnis, Inmami Shi'a, Ismaili Shi'a, and Sufis. Key to the rebels' success were such intangible factors as their unswerving devotion to their faith, quite apart from their strong commitment to preserve regional (much less national) independence.
(© Pascal Manoukian/Sygma/Corbis)

together with Soviet Bloc munitions and firearms purchased in vast quantities by the United States and other nations wishing to conceal the source of the donations.

In three separate forays deep into Afghan territory, mostly on foot and horseback, Bonner recorded regular observations about the motivations behind the mujahideen, the hardships they endured, and the character of their personnel. Bonner found these extraordinary fighting men more than capable of managing in the field without the amenities of an industrialized society. Life in Afghanistan demanded hardiness, and faith in Islam buoyed up and encouraged a people already toughened by a harsh climate and landscape, as well as by scratching out an existence on herding and modest agricultural yields.

During the course of his travels, Bonner identified religion as the prime mover of these 'fighters for the faith'. He noted:

There are few medics for the wounded ... no pensions for the disabled. All that doesn't matter. The Afghans say they are fighting a jihad, a holy war, and call themselves mujahidin, holy warriors. The old and the young, the strong and even the disabled say they will fight on to the next generation if necessary. (Bonner 1987: 2)

Numerous fighters, regardless of faction or geographical region, confirmed the fact, one resistance commander assuring him: 'We know our country will be free some day ... We will not be discouraged. We will fight until we have an Islamic government in Afghanistan' (Bonner 1987: 71). Another chorused the same basic message: 'We fight for God and our country and for our country's freedom' (Bonner 1987: 72). Another announced defiantly: 'If only one *mujahid* is left alive, he will fight the Russians' (Bonner 1987: 72). The youngest fighters shared the views of their elders: a Kalashnikov-wielding 15-year-old boy from Mazar-e Sharif told Bonner: 'God is with us and we are sure we will make the Russians leave our country' (Bonner 1987: 175).

The fighters Bonner encountered varied considerably in age, from a 13-year-old who displayed a grenade once thrown at him that failed to explode, to bearded old men with two generations of their families living in filthy refugee camps in Pakistan. In general, he found commanders charismatic and respected, yet shunning the outward symbols of rank, designating themselves merely 'commander' irrespective of the size of their following, which could range from a few dozen lightly equipped men to hundreds of fighters bearing assault rifles, RPGs and heavy machine guns. One leader, Abdul Wahab, aged 31, Bonner found

... always busy, conferring with the squad leaders or doing paper work with clerks. He was the epitome of a tough, resourceful, mujahidin commander. In another army he might have had the bars of a captain on his shoulders, but the Afghans, with their intense individuality and their inability to tolerate superiority in others, have organized their army without a show of uniforms or a clear designation of rank ... Leaders are distinguished not by symbols on their shoulders but by how they act and what they are able to accomplish – in battle or ... in getting a large number of unruly Afghans armed, fed, and across the mountains ... (Bonner 1987: 102)

Bonner and the group he accompanied came under attack on only one, harrowing, occasion:

The high ground was like the rear tier of an amphitheatre, looking across to the battle on the hill above Nargasay village [in Paktia province]. A pair of MiGs appeared. Twin white vapour trails in the blue sky signalled that a pilot had fired a pair of rockets. They slammed into the hill and the pilot pulled out of his dive, banking over our heads for another run. Soon the second MiG rocketed and banked away. A helicopter gun ship approached. It hovered over the hill, raining bullets down on the mujahidin among the rocks. Mortar shells whooshed and exploded with a thumping sound. A pall of smoke and dust drifted over the valley.

The staccato of Kalashnikov shots, and single shots from rifles, gradually subsided, and the MiGs and helicopters flew away. Silence returned, but the mujahidin remained hidden in case there was another attack. The dust settled

... Out of nowhere, a rocket slammed into the ground about 150 feet in front of me. Another struck with a crash and a shower of stones. Shocked, I ran back to the trees. (Bonner 1987: 16–17)

During a second expedition into Afghanistan, also in 1985, Bonner arranged to accompany a resistance group bound for Jegdalek, in Kabul province. They began their long, extremely arduous journey just across the border in Parachinar, Pakistan, where the shops openly sold weapons:

... arrays of light machine guns, Kalashnikovs, rifles, and pistols; boxes and tins of bullets, grenades, and shells; and heaps of bandoliers and canvas ammunition holders all looked alike. The more costly items, like mortars and shoulder-fired, rocket-propelled grenade antitank weapons, called RPG-7s, were kept out of sight in the back of a store ... A burst of rifle fire from the open area in back of the shops, and even the sharp explosion of a shell, was testimony that something had been bought and was being tested. (Bonner 1987: 55–56)

Provided with a packhorse without the benefit of stirrups and loaded with baggage atop which he uncomfortably perched, Bonner placed a blanket on his head and, leaving only his eyes exposed, stepped across the border near Teri Mangal without interference from border officials, who often exacted bribes to ensure passage across the poorly monitored frontier. On the first day he discovered the trail marked by a destroyed Afghan border post, the hulk of a Soviet tank stripped of its wheels for scrap metal and the deserted remains of a village, with the skeletons of seven tanks and APCs littering the area – all thought to date from the initial days of the invasion more than five years earlier.

His legs ached from being spread out over the packs and sometimes obliged him to dismount in order to walk, which in the event offered little relief and annoyed his hosts, who insisted he ride to keep up. So directed, Bonner and the others ascended a mountain with a trail that narrowed to

An Afghan girl. Although most girls enter wedlock between the ages of 15 to 17, it is not unknown for children of 12 or 13 to marry, complete with a 'bride price' (*shir-baha* in Dari; *wulwar* in Pushtu) consisting of a payment made to her relatives by the groom's family. Bride price functions as a form of economic exchange, compensating the girl's family for the loss of a financially valuable asset, since the payment of money or provision of livestock, or both, cushions the loss of her labour. By contrast, a dowry (*jahiz* in Dari; *khawkul* in Pushtu) may be provided to the groom's family, sometimes equivalent to the bride price, and may include clothing, household goods or other items useful to the newly married couple. (© Reza/Webistan/Corbis)

no more than 2ft in width – just enough space, as far as he reckoned, for his horse to keep a proper footing along the precipice, over which lay 'a void, with a dizzying drop below' (Bonner 1987: 59). Trembling with cold amid the snowy landscape, he debated whether to close his eyes to ignore the danger or to maintain his weary gaze through the gloom so as to be prepared when he tumbled to oblivion.

Journeys like these became a regular feature of Bonner's experiences in Afghanistan. He ascended mountain paths reaching over 5,000ft, with the ground beneath him hard with frost and

weeks of similar hardships yet to endure before reaching his destination. His group stopped at shabby guesthouses, plunging to the floor utterly exhausted after eight, ten or 12 hours' movement at a stint, only to rise again early each morning, fortified with nothing more than bread and greasy potatoes or some other improvised nourishment – which Bonner found incapable of properly sustaining him as his bedraggled, sore-covered horse struggled to convey him through sub-zero temperatures and amidst impossible altitudes.

One evening, at the top of a steep rise, they could dimly make out in the valley beneath them the town of Jegdalek, a place near the scene of the destruction of the ill-fated Anglo-Indian army during its retreat from Kabul to Jalalabad in 1842. But the Afghans never judged distance with any interest in achieving accuracy, as Bonner and other Western contemporaries noted; there was still a considerable distance to go.

Night fell and clouds obscured the moon. We went up another mountain, the darkened trail narrower than it had been the day before. I was aware of the abyss yawning at my side, but I kept telling myself to trust the horse … Then we started down an almost vertical slope … Suddenly we were on a narrow ledge with a door leading into a room in a mountain hut. I stumbled in and lay on the ground, numb from the journey: thirteen hours on foot and horseback, with an hour's break for lunch, capped by the final half-hour rush in the dark over rocks and down the cliff. (Bonner 1987: 62)

They eventually reached Jegdalek, once boasting a population of about 5,000, only to discover it deserted and in ruins. The debris of war littered the ground, including cluster bombs, fragments of missiles, and pieces of the anti-personnel mines that the Russians had fashioned into objects resembling clocks, watches and pens before dropping them from helicopters with the intention of attracting children's attention. Those aware of the danger threw stones at them to make them explode.

Others, unaware of the mines' presence or ignorant of their danger, lost limbs – or their lives.

On a final journey, after the snows had melted and opened a route through a different set of mountains, Bonner joined a large convoy of men and arms bound for Mazar-e Sharif. He took particular interest in the array of modern weaponry the mujahideen managed to acquire – impressive, yet transported in the most rudimentary, unsophisticated fashion:

… tin containers of ammunition, wooden boxes of mortar shells, dozens of Chinese mines, plastic tubes encasing antitank grenades, bundles of rocket charges for these grenades, mortars, several Dashika [DShK] heavy machine guns with large tripod mounts, a shoulder-operated recoilless rifle … and bales of rough gray blankets and khaki jackets. Some of the men divided the unloaded supplies into portions and tied them into pairs of wide-woven rope nets that could be lifted up and slung over the back of an animal, with an even balance on either side. Others opened some of the ammunition tins and packed the clips of their Kalashnikovs and the belts and feeder boxes for light machine guns. (Bonner 1987: 105)

Crossing seemingly endless mountains, they eventually found road transport, even as a small donkey loaded with ammunition began to lose its footing and slumped to the ground from exhaustion. Travelling in the dark posed some of the worst of many dangers, he recalled:

… we started, zigzagging through bomb holes and the craters left by mine explosions, bumping over dirt and rocks from landslides, skirting a chasm where a side of the road had collapsed into the valley below and, at one point, inching our way across a concrete bridge with a huge gap torn from the side. All along the way were the ancient hulks of Soviet tanks and armored cars. (Bonner 1987: 110–11)

They eventually reached their destination, encountering *en route* all manner of cut-throats and miscreants, including rival resistance groups who tried to rob them of their weapons and ammunition, DRA defectors, and Soviet deserters inducted into the service of the mujahideen after voluntary conversion to Islam.

Bonner eventually returned to New York, published his stories and later wrote a full-scale account of his experiences. His is one of several insightful records left by the handful of Western journalists who, in braving the myriad dangers of Afghanistan, helped through their reminiscences to shed light on a war that went largely unreported in the West – where few observers appreciated the profound impact the conflict was to have, not merely on the participants themselves, but on those whose interests years later would draw them into the region, especially the United States.

UN diplomacy and Soviet withdrawal

Over time neither overwhelming military force nor the internal reforms undertaken by the Soviets and their Afghan protégés could hope to crush the insurgency. While some Afghans, particularly those in the cities and above all the educated classes, collaborated with the Soviets, DRA forces stood distinctively subordinate to their counterparts. In that role, given their consistently poor operational record,

Soviets departing Afghanistan in February 1989, probably from Bagram air base. Subjugating a small, underdeveloped but exceedingly martial country proved a far greater endeavour than the Soviets ever imagined. At the time of the invasion they took a keen interest in the internal affairs of developing nations, believing all to be 'ripe for socialism' such as Eastern Europe, parts of Latin America and Africa. The fact that the Soviet leadership failed to anticipate the Afghan people's reaction to their invasion also goes far in explaining its foolish decision to cross the border in December 1979. (© Patrick Robert/Sygma/Corbis)

morale necessarily suffered and declined. Neither Soviet nor Afghan leaders could offer a political solution to continued resistance, and with an impasse in the field stretching far longer than ever anticipated, stirrings in Moscow began to encourage withdrawal, not least because the mujahideen demonstrated no inclination to negotiate under circumstances where compromise offered them nothing.

Accordingly, Moscow began to appreciate in 1985 that the war had become unwinnable. Chernenko and Andropov, both of whom succeeded Brezhnev as party secretary for brief periods (November 1982–February 1984 and February 1984–March 1985 respectively), suffered from ill health during their entire periods in office, during which they failed to exercise the energy and leadership required to keep the insurgency under

control, much less destroy it. This obliged the Central Committee to appoint a younger man to finish the job. Coming to power on 10 March 1985, Mikhail Gorbachev inherited an intractable war, as the chief of the Soviet General Staff, Marshal Sergei Akhromeyev (1923–91), explained:

In the past seven years Soviet soldiers have had their boots on the ground in every square kilometre of the country. But as soon as they left, the enemy returned and restored everything the way it was before. We have lost this war. The majority of the Afghan people support the counter-revolution. We have lost the peasantry, who have got nothing from the revolution. 80% of the country is in the hands of the counter-revolution. And the position of the peasants there is better than it is on the territory controlled by the government. (Quoted in Johnson 2011: 241)

Gorbachev represented a fresh start in Soviet foreign policy as well as in domestic politics. He was a leader whose policy of *glasnost* (openness) had from the beginning of his time in office already tolerated internal – and even public – criticism of the war, and who recognized the strategic errors committed by his country. His desire to extricate troops from Afghanistan centred on three key motives. First and foremost, the failing prospects of the war rendered further operations pointless. Second, withdrawal would provide a mechanism by which to improve the Soviet Union's relations with the West, particularly with the United States at a time when the issue of nuclear disarmament remained high on both countries' agendas. Indeed, even if the Carter administration's (1977–81) boycott of the 1980 Moscow Olympics and the embargo of American grain shipments to the Soviet Union had constituted nothing more than irritation, Carter's and the subsequent Reagan administration's (1981–89) refusal to continue talks to try to ratify the proposed SALT II restrictions on nuclear weapons stood indefinitely postponed as a result of the invasion, and Gorbachev could

Soviet soldier handling supplies at Kabul Airport. Historically, such troops engaged in high-tempo, large-scale conventional operations to achieve success. In sharp contrast, the war in Afghanistan involved low-level tactics, best conducted by highly mobile units led by platoon, not divisional, commanders with doctrine suited to the fluid nature of asymmetric warfare. By the time Soviet tactics evolved to adapt to these very different circumstances the war was already effectively lost. (© Patrick Robert/Sygma/Corbis)

countenance this no longer. Third, with domestic discontent partly assuaged by the troops' return and military expenditure reduced, he could concentrate on the social, economic and political reforms urgently needed within the USSR.

The origins of the decision to withdraw require brief examination. Anatoly Dobrynin (1919–2010), the Soviet ambassador to the United States between 1962 and 1986, claimed that at a Politburo meeting of 17 October 1985 Gorbachev declared, 'it's time to leave', to which the other members raised no objection. They fixed no date for final withdrawal, but the die had been cast. Debate continues about the degree to which this meeting represented the first concrete decision to bring an end to the war, but any doubts may be cast aside by the decisive results of the Politburo meeting held on 13 November 1986, in which Akhromeyev made a devastatingly

According to the Brezhnev Doctrine, all socialist states shared a common responsibility to oppose threats to socialism in any other like-minded state. This factor, amongst others, helped propel the Soviet Union into the Afghan quagmire. Gorbachev, seen here in Paris in 1985, recognized the folly of this adventure, appreciating that, ideologically speaking, the war did not conform to Marxist–Leninist doctrine, since the Soviets could not conceive of a popular war waged against a regime ostensibly representing their interests. (© Peter Turnley/Corbis)

prescient and unchallengeable assertion: 'we have lost the battle for the Afghan people'. Accordingly, Gorbachev proposed that the Soviet Union should withdraw its forces over a two-year period, with half removed in 1987 and the rest to leave the following year, a recommendation to which the other members gave their assent. Here stood the idea in principle; now Gorbachev needed the mechanism by which to implement it.

To lay the groundwork for troop withdrawal, Soviet authorities sought to expand DRA forces to enable them to take a more active combat role. However, this did not achieve the desired effect, since government military personnel continued to perform unreliably against their compatriots in the resistance, leaving Soviet troops to continue to bear the greatest burden in combat. This compounded anxiety over the likelihood of a smooth transition of security affairs to the Kabul regime, already looking grim in light of Najibullah's continuing failure successfully to implement his programme of reforms. Gennady Bocharov was probably not alone in expressing anxiety about the competence of the Soviet advisors serving in Kabul. While he acknowledged that some Central Asian specialists served in Afghanistan, most were merely city and regional party secretaries:

They knew absolutely nothing about the east. Their conception of Afghanistan was hazy, to say the least … but the standard party advisers dealt with practical matters. They were not interested in consultations. As for those who were charged with devising strategy and tactics – they frankly ignored the opinions of any specialist …

The trouble with the advisers was not just that they didn't know Afghanistan. They did not know something even more important: how to run things in their own backyard, let alone a foreign country. (Bocharov 1990: 61)

In short, it became clear that Moscow would eventually have to withdraw from Afghanistan in as honourable a fashion as possible and thus leave Najibullah to his own devices, albeit heavily subsidized with food, weapons and matériel.

The United Nations stood as the obvious intermediary between the belligerents. Gorbachev depended on it to achieve this role, with the Afghan government effectively representing Soviet interests and Pakistan acting on behalf of the mujahideen, since Islamabad unofficially supported the resistance, while the United States by extension supported the same through Pakistan. As such, negotiations conducted by the United Nations, if successful, stood to benefit the interests of all the principal parties to the conflict, belligerents and non-belligerents alike. Having said this, accords brokered by the UN necessarily set some limitations on its freedom of action in light of the Soviet Union's position as a permanent member of the Security Council. That fact had protected the aggressor in 1979, since the Soviet Union could veto the UN's original condemnation of its invasion. Now, nearly a decade later, for the sake of extricating themselves from an unwinnable war, the Soviets were happily prepared to regard the UN as a third party in the process of 'conflict resolution' by accepting its 'good offices' and the shuttle diplomacy it could offer. Specifically, the Secretary General, by the authority of the UN, could engage in negotiations unilaterally, supported by the UN Secretariat.

The Geneva Accords were signed on 14 April 1988, by which the Soviets agreed to remove their forces from Afghanistan. Other essential elements established for Afghanistan and Pakistan a policy of mutual non-interference and non-intervention with respect to sovereignty, economic stability and territorial integrity. According to one section of Article II, neither side could train, equip, finance or recruit mercenaries, whatever their origin, for the purpose of engaging in hostile activity in either party's territory, including the maintenance of bases for purposes of supporting outside forces. As such, the DRA was to be left to its own devices with respect

to subduing its own domestic insurgency and could not accept foreign intervention, though this did not preclude money and weapons.

For the various parties concerned, this represented a reasonable outcome, notwithstanding the fact that no delegates directly represented the mujahideen. Attempting to negotiate with the disparate groups that comprised the resistance – represented by seven different political parties, all based in Pakistan – would probably have been futile, as any accord would inevitably have required separate agreements with rival groups, a course almost certain to prolong the conflict and lead to fighting between factions within the mujahideen competing for power in a post-communist Afghanistan. But while the settlement enabled the Soviets to claim that they had finally accorded with international calls for their withdrawal, they obviously

The Geneva Peace Accords, concluded in 1988, enabled the Soviets to begin the process of withdrawing their troops, leaving behind a friendly, well-funded and well-equipped regime in Kabul to carry on the fight against the mujahideen. For years, ordinary Soviet citizens had simply not understood why the government conscripted young men for service in a far-off land whose politics appeared to have no bearing on Soviet security. (© Thierry Orban/Sygma/Corbis)

President Najibullah, seen here in Kabul in May 1988, exercised poor control over Afghanistan and could not lead an autonomous government without continued Soviet support in the form of weapons, supplies and funds. While Kabul continued to enjoy some legitimate basis for rule via local and regional commanders, no effective, properly integrated structures at the national level existed with which Afghans could identify, much less respect. Against the backdrop of political illegitimacy and military failure in the field over many years, the DRA regime faced an increasingly poor prospect of clinging to power. (© Patrick Robert/Sygma/Corbis)

France, Britain, Japan and Italy. The United States withdrew its diplomatic staff three days later, only reopening its embassy in December 2001 when its troops retook Kabul from the Taliban in the wake of the 9/11 bombings. Meanwhile, the passing of Soviet troops back over the border went largely unchallenged by the resistance, though the Soviets themselves, anxious to prevent attacks on their forces as they withdrew, staged a campaign of terror, largely with concentrated artillery fire, against villages along their route towards the frontier so as to intimidate the mujahideen into restraint. Thousands streamed away from their villages as vast Soviet columns trundled through the smoke of the devastation left in their wake. Finally, on 15 February, General Boris Gromov, commander of the 40th Army and the last Soviet soldier to leave the country, crossed the bridge at Termez, so putting an end to a tragic adventure fraught with human folly and misguided ambition.

In the immediate wake of the Soviets' departure the mujahideen largely ceased their operations, preserving and expanding their resources and manpower for the day when they would oppose other factions vying for sole control of government machinery in Kabul. Civil war was encouraged by the fact that rival groups expected some influence on the war's outcome in compensation for the effort expended since its beginning. Indeed, internecine fighting was bound to continue until a sole victor emerged. Any power-sharing was unlikely, for competing factions possessed no mechanism for building trust between rivals, and no agreement existed to divide responsibility for the rebuilding of the country's devastated infrastructure, for control over the military and security forces, or for the distribution of political power, amongst many other issues. As a natural consequence of these and many other factors, the fighting continued for another three years, mostly against the government, but with some clashes between insurgent groups. During this period the Soviets continued to fund Najibullah's government, leaving in its

could not ensure a peaceful outcome between their surrogates in Kabul and the resistance. Thus, the Geneva Accords merely brought to a close one dimension of the Afghan civil war. If anything, every prospect still existed for that bitter struggle to continue in the wake of Soviet withdrawal, a struggle that, it is important to recall, had begun in 1978 before the Soviet invasion (though some may argue the insurgency properly dated from Daoud's accession to power in 1973).

The withdrawal signalled the international isolation of Najibullah's regime, formalized when diplomats from key Western nations closed their embassies in Kabul. West Germany began the process on 21 January 1989, followed on the 27th by hands an enormous stockpile of weapons and ammunition that enabled the president to maintain his increasingly tenuous grip on power. But that is to anticipate events: in the post-withdrawal period the Soviet Union established the greatest air-bridge since the Berlin Blockade of 1948, furnishing aid to the DRA estimated at a staggering $300 million a month, with one report indicating that weapons alone delivered in the six months after February 1989 carried a value of $1.4 billion.

However, matters continued to deteriorate for the Afghan regime, a fact underscored by the attempted coup staged by General Shah Nawaz Tenai (1950–) in April 1990, after which Najibullah understandably took an increasingly dim view of the loyalty of his security forces, which declined in strength from as many as 400,000 (including army, paramilitary police and KhAD) in 1989 to 160,000 in 1991. His subsequent actions betrayed a man narrowly clinging to power. After his desperate appeals to rural leaders for stability and co-operation were rejected, he turned to raising sizeable militias to achieve the objectives that his unreliable regular forces could not. In Herat, a hotbed of resistance, government militia increased from about 14,000 in 1986 to 70,000 in 1991, largely through attractive offers of arms and money to mujahideen leaders prepared to defect with their fighters to the government now that the Soviet threat had passed and Kabul could supply their needs. A fifth of former mujahideen groups shifted to the government side and recast themselves as government militia, while a further 40 per cent accepted offers of a ceasefire. The rest remained irreconcilable. Ironically, these new units proved to be the president's undoing, for they grew so large – 170,000 in 1991, accounting for over 50 per cent of government forces – as to become practically self-governing in their own areas of operation, and when with the collapse of the Soviet Union Moscow immediately ceased funding the DRA, the various militias refused to obey orders from Najibullah's now transparently tottering

Communists of the PDPA demonstrating in Kabul in February 1989. The short-term causes of the war may be dated from the communist-led military coup of April 1978, after which the new head of state, Nur Mohammed Taraki, began to implement sweeping Marxist reforms to alter the status of women, redistribute land and overhaul the Afghan social structure, all changes which met substantial opposition across large swathes of the conservative, tribal-based countryside. (© Patrick Robert/Sygma/Corbis)

regime. In many cases these rogue forces established themselves as independent units under the more powerful militia commanders who fashioned themselves into warlords. Some of these controlled extensive areas almost as fiefdoms, collecting taxes and administering their own laws, and operating in an increasingly chaotic and unstable state. Less powerful militia groups mimicked this practice, either vying for control over smaller areas theoretically under government authority or over other militia groups. In so doing they inaugurated a new period of the existing civil war that followed the fall of Najibullah's regime in April 1992, and which continued even after the Taliban seized Kabul in 1996, by which time the loss in human life may even have exceeded that of the period of Soviet occupation.

Conclusion and consequences

Impact on the Soviet Union

Earlier chapters have revealed the Soviets' many military shortcomings in frank terms. It is now time to examine the effects of those shortcomings on the troops themselves and to assess the political impact of the war on the USSR.

Statistics connected with the Soviets' role in the war make for depressing reading. Total forces deployed over the whole course of the conflict amounted to approximately

Mujahideen fighters struggle for control of Kabul in April 1992. For the Soviets, the war ended on 15 February 1989 when the last of their troops pulled out of Afghanistan, but this did not mark the end of the fighting amongst the Afghans themselves. After Najibullah's regime fell, the civil war continued for another four years until the Taliban emerged triumphant. (© Kapoor Baldev/Sygma/Corbis)

642,000 personnel. Of these, approximately 545,000 served in the regular forces, while another 90,000 came from armed KGB units. Perhaps 5,000 belonged to the MVD (*Ministerstvo Vnutrennikh Del* or Ministry of Internal Affairs). Statistics for the dead and missing vary according to the source consulted, but range between 13,000 and 15,000 personnel. 10,751 soldiers became invalids, many as amputees. Yet these already substantial figures must be seen in light of the 469,685 sick and wounded – or over 70 per cent of the total force – discharged and repatriated. Statistics for those stricken with disease tell an even more revealing story: a staggering 415,932, of whom 115,308 men suffered from infectious hepatitis and 31,080 from typhoid fever. The sheer scale of this suffering reveals the dreadful state of hygiene prevalent within the Soviet forces and their

appalling conditions in the field. The pressure on Soviet hospitals – particularly with respect to the long-term sick and the disabled – can only be reckoned to have been enormous, with correspondingly serious social implications for society as a whole. In sharp contrast to their fathers who had defended the country against the German menace during World War II, soldiers returning from Afghanistan not only received no hero's welcome but often felt shunned by a public detached from, if not actually hostile to, the war. The loss in matériel and hardware also helps place in perspective the scale of the conflict, and offers a sharp lesson to those who would slavishly depend on technology alone as some sort of magical recipe for success: 118 jets, 333 helicopters, 147 tanks, 1,314 armoured personnel carriers, 433 artillery pieces and mortars, 1,138 radio sets and CP vehicles, 510 engineering vehicles and 11,369 trucks.

There is no question that the Soviet war effort suffered from poor or virtually non-existent political direction. The series of either ineffective political masters in Moscow or the regularity with which they sickened and died off during the 1980s contributed in no small way towards Soviet failure. Brezhnev, not healthy at the time of the invasion, became incapacitated the following year and did not succumb to his illness until November 1982, leaving all decisions to committees exercising collective leadership. His successor, Yuri Andropov, lasted less than two years, and upon his death in February 1984 Konstantin Chernenko carried on for little more than a year until his own demise. During this whole period the conflict was allowed to carry on with little in the way of decision-making over substantial issues concerning the conduct of operations or the overall objective of the war. When at last Gorbachev took the helm and found that the war could not be brought to a conclusion within a year – in fact Soviet casualties rose to record levels during that period – he sought a means to withdraw

in a dignified fashion, which as we have seen the United Nations provided.

Even before the troops returned the impact of the war at home had become palpable. The Soviet military experience in Afghanistan amounted to a slow, attritional effort, which not only demonstrated the declining combat effectiveness of the USSR's armed forces, but revealed stark, irreparable cracks developing within the Soviet political infrastructure. Society itself underwent change owing to the rotation in and out of Afghanistan of conscripted troops, whose disappointments, stories of hardship and frustration permeated Soviet society, undermining morale and sowing seeds of doubt respecting both the war effort and also the people's confidence in the political and economic system as a whole. Thus, problems experienced in Afghanistan manifested themselves back home, or one could contend that internal disintegration reflected on Soviet troops' morale in theatre. The two, in any event, proved mutually destructive, albeit within a process that must be seen as gradual, like that of the growing body count of the war.

While only a small percentage of the population served in the war or was touched by it as a consequence of the loss of a son, brother or husband, the Soviet experience in Afghanistan created a large body of disaffected veterans of the conflict. Known as the *afgantsy*, these veterans' disillusionment at home manifested itself over a range of emotions, from unexpressed derision of Moscow to outright criticism of the Soviet system in general. Such veterans did not organize themselves into any form of political movement or lobby, but in light of Gorbachev's growing liberalization of Soviet society as a consequence of his policies of *glasnost* ('openness') and *perestroika* (literally 're-structuring', involving wholesale changes to the Soviet state), the attitudes of Afghan veterans nevertheless played some part in influencing public opinion and contributing to the general atmosphere of disgruntled citizens now prepared to question decisions

An Afghan refugee family on the move. Of the country's pre-war population of about 15 million, a third became refugees in Pakistan and Iran, accounting for half the world's refugees at that time, in addition to perhaps a million internally displaced people. No one suffered more than ordinary civilian Afghans. The population of Kabul felt the impact of war comparatively less owing to the Soviets' virtually complete control of major metropolitan centres, but rural dwellers had always remained most vulnerable to Soviet and DRA forces. (© Reza/Webistan/Corbis)

intervention in Afghanistan, prompting those of a reformist disposition to use the failing military effort as a means to push through their agendas and thus speed the process of change. Many analysts point to the declining Soviet economy, the inability of the state to continue to bear the burden of subsidizing communist allies around the world, Afghanistan included, and the impossibility of trying to match the United States in the nuclear arms race as the prime movers in the collapse of the Soviet Union.

In the end the Soviets had intervened on the basis of supporting a notionally communist state; in reality, from 1978 the succession of Afghan regimes only attracted widespread domestic condemnation followed by open hostility and civil war. The fact of Soviet withdrawal in 1989 – with little to show for it but a deeply unpopular satellite government condemned to hold down an insurgency that even the Soviets had failed to contain, much less defeat – went far in eroding the long-held Soviet doctrine that socialism represented a positive and irreversible movement for the political, social and economic good of peoples across the globe.

made at all levels of government, including the Kremlin. In short, the war became a metaphor for systemic problems within Soviet society, and thus accelerated the rate of social and political change under way since Gorbachev came to power in the spring of 1985. The cost of the war exacerbated such problems, for expenditure ran into the billions and placed an enormous strain on the Soviet economy, which continued with the flow of supplies to Najibullah's regime after the troops returned home.

Criticism of communist rule, or at least its existing form, also developed from within, for the war led to a loss of faith in the party leadership amongst the middle and upper echelons of the Communist Party itself. Whereas before and during the Brezhnev era the party elite tended to operate on the basis of intra-party consultation, this practice had rapidly declined during the years of

Impact on Afghanistan

Statistics vary on the unnatural, war-related Afghan deaths that occurred during the Soviet occupation, but range from between 900,000 to 1.3 million people. What proportion of this number may be identified as mujahideen is impossible to discern, but their losses must have numbered in the many tens of thousands. Yet this already staggering scale of combined military and civilian fatalities must not obscure the record of suffering caused to ordinary villagers through injury and disability. An estimated 1.5 million Afghan civilians became physically disabled as a result of the war. In addition, the psychological trauma caused by the conflict was both unquantifiable and virtually untreatable in the 1980s in a country bereft of facilities or suitable personnel, not to mention a prevailing culture that does not recognize depression properly and stigmatizes those who fail to conceal the trauma associated with that condition. The Soviets also sowed and left behind millions of mines, which continue to kill and maim. On the basis of these bare facts, the damage and suffering inflicted on Afghanistan exceeds that meted out by the Germans on the Soviets between 1941 and 1945. This speaks volumes for the colossal scale of this tragedy.

Vast numbers of Afghans became displaced as a result of the war, with over 6 million refugees – at least a third of the pre-war population – living under miserable conditions beyond Afghanistan's borders in Iran and Pakistan by the early 1990s. Most benefited to some extent from the efforts of both the Pakistani and Iranian authorities to provide aid to this massive influx of people, but in the end the absence of these refugees from their villages left large numbers of people without skills otherwise acquired and practised in farming and cottage-industry activity. Quite apart from those already possessing some skills, young

people found themselves denied the ability to learn a trade, engage in agriculture or to manage and herd livestock. To this huge number of external refugees must be added those internally displaced, an estimated two million people. The population of Kabul grew enormously as rural dwellers flocked to the capital in search of protection from air attack in the countryside. Women and children suffered particularly badly, since while their menfolk were away serving in government units or as resistance fighters, they were left to manage for themselves in the devastation caused by aerial mines and high explosives scattered over and around mud-brick homes and compounds whose simple structures offered no protection from such ordnance. Quite apart from the social

An Uzbek woman looks for her son amongst returning troops in Termez in March 1989. The Soviets achieved almost nothing in exchange for nine years' costly effort, having spent billions and sacrificed the lives of thousands of their soldiers. Growing disillusionment amongst Soviet citizens had, in the end, impaired public faith in the government's capacity to manage foreign policy and generally to pursue the welfare of the nation. (© Reuters/Corbis)

Wrecked vehicles and helmets left behind in the wake of withdrawal. The Soviets' failure derived partly from the political hubris of politicians, who grievously underestimated the colossal scale of the enterprise on which they had embarked in 1979 and who failed to establish what has since become known as an 'exit strategy'. The chronic shortage of men, equipment and supplies, amongst other factors, proved fatal to their ambitions. (© Reuters/Corbis)

isolation which arose, women suffered from the loss of the wages their husbands normally brought home to feed families in a society where the long-term absence or death of a father and or his sons could produce serious disruption to family life, financially as well as socially.

Apart from the damage inflicted on the population, the war saw severe disruption to the Afghan economy, largely through the physical effects of bombing and artillery fire. The Soviets sought out targets representing important elements of the country's infrastructure, while the absence of regular maintenance left other elements useless after years of neglect, owing to lack of parts or the

absence of trained personnel to maintain machinery. As discussed, mud-brick housing offered no protection against high explosives, whether delivered on the ground or in the air, with the result that by the early 1990s, 60 per cent of schools did not possess a physical structure. The country already lacked a railway system and boasted little more than a rudimentary road network, apart from the massive ring road that the Americans had built long before the war. What remained deteriorated during the 1980s, in turn adversely affecting trade and thus the economy as a whole, quite apart from making refugees' journeys all the more arduous. Moreover, general destruction, attributable to both sides, accounted for the loss of more than 1,800 schools, 31 hospitals, 11 health centres, and 14,000 kilometres of telephone cable.

The war also severely disrupted agriculture, the mainstay of the country's economy, to a great extent. While prior to the coup in 1978 Afghanistan unquestionably passed as a poor country, it did not qualify as one suffering from hunger. By 1987, however, this had changed, since agricultural output had sharply declined to only a third of 1978 figures as a result of the loss of land suitable for cultivation, a decline by a half of land once available for cultivation but now unusable owing, for instance, to the wide-scale deaths of draught oxen. The bombardment of hundreds of villages and wide areas of cultivated land in order to force the population off the land and into the cities – or in any event away from areas considered vital to the Soviets – accounted for much of this deliberately inflicted damage.

Afghanistan also suffered a severe decline in its balance of payments owing to a sharp rise in imports and a contrasting fall in exports. The country's trade deficit rose in 1980 from $69 million – representing 9.8 per cent of exports – to $649 million or 276.2 per cent of exports ten years later. Foreign debt also rose from $1.2 billion in 1980 to $5.1 billion a decade on. Inflation soared, with an increase of 980 per cent during the 1980s. All these statistics translated into the reality of a sharp decline in the standard of living, with progressively higher prices for imported goods as the Afghan currency fell in value, in turn causing families to struggle against impossible odds to feed themselves and their children amidst all the other consequences of the war.

Final words

The Soviet–Afghan War demonstrated that the Soviets had embarked on an adventure based on unattainable goals. They sought to uphold a manifestly weak and unpopular government and in so doing, especially after violating Afghan soil, shattered any degree of legitimacy that the regime might have hoped to garner from the Afghan people. When Taraki's communist regime came to power in Kabul in 1978 it failed to recognize that the bulk of Afghan society, based as it was on tribal structures with nothing in common with Marxist ideology, did not desire fundamental change to its way of life, not least reforms foisted upon it from outside that represented a direct threat to centuries of tradition and religious conviction. Thus, when the Kabul regime and its PDPA apparatus, activists, functionaries and KhAD agents spread across the country with revolutionary fervour, they unwittingly propelled Afghanistan into civil war, with Soviet intervention to prop up the regime exponentially worsening the existing domestic strife to appalling levels of misery and physical devastation, splitting the country along even deeper factional lines than before and encouraging Islamic extremism to boot.

The British Army field manual, *Countering Insurgency*, concisely sums up Soviet errors:

Soviet activity failed due to several key strategic factors:

- *They failed to remove the extensive external support provided to the Mujahideen;*
- *Inability of the Soviets to exploit internal weaknesses among the insurgents;*

- *Absence of a stable government in Kabul commanding popular respect.*

The Soviets failed to adopt an effective counter-insurgency strategy:

- *There was no integration of military and political objectives and tactics;*
- *[No] immediate exploitation of intelligence;*
- *They focused almost exclusively on search and destroy operations;*
- *They had no understanding of the local community;*
- *They failed to restrict the enemy supply lines and communications networks.*

Numerical superiority was lacking – an estimated Soviet and Afghan Government force of 400,000–500,000 was required.

Endurance, will and moral commitment were lacking. (MoD 2010: Section 3-15)

The war also revealed, as had Vietnam for the Americans 20 years earlier, that victory remains elusive even for a superpower when it confronts an opponent driven by deep ideological or religious convictions and bolstered morally, but above all materially, by generous external allies. Like the Vietminh and Viet Cong in the 1950s and '60s, the mujahideen proved themselves an exceedingly formidable force to reckon with, notwithstanding their initial acute deficiencies in weapons, ammunition and supplies. Once adequately armed, equipped and fed, and with limited access to safe havens providing training and rest, the motivation and drive of an exceptionally robust, utterly determined, ideologically driven foe employing tactics suited to the circumstances produced the most intractable of opponents: one with time on his side and a willingness to accept horrific losses many times in excess of his adversary. Here lay the ingredients of the Soviet Union's military demise and the concomitant ruins of its political ambitions in the region.

Bibliography and further reading

Alexiev, Alex, *Inside the Soviet Army in Afghanistan* (Rand Corporation, 1988)

Alexievich, Svetlana, *Zinky Boys: Soviet Voices from a Forgotten War* (Chatto & Windus, 1992)

Anderson, Jon Lee, *Guerrilla: Journeys in the Insurgent World* (Abacus, 2006)

Arnold, Anthony, *Afghanistan: The Soviet Invasion in Perspective* (Hoover Institution Press, 1985)

Arnold, Anthony, *The Fateful Pebble: Afghanistan's Role in the Fall of the Soviet Empire* (Presidio Press, 1993)

Aspaturian, Dallin, et al., *The Soviet Invasion of Afghanistan: Three Perspectives* (University of California Press, 1996)

Barfield, Thomas, *Afghanistan: A Cultural and Political History* (Princeton UP, 2012)

Bocharov, Gennady, *Russian Roulette: Afghanistan through Russian Eyes* (HarperCollins, 1990)

Bonner, Arthur, *Among the Afghans* (Duke UP, 1987)

Borer, Douglas, *Superpowers Defeated: Vietnam and Afghanistan Compared* (Routledge, 1999)

Borovik, Artyom, *The Hidden War: A Russian Journalist's Account of the Soviet War in Afghanistan* (Faber & Faber, 2001)

Bradsher, Henry, *Afghanistan and the Soviet Union* (Duke UP, 1983)

Bradsher, Henry, *Afghan Communism and Soviet Intervention* (OUP, 1999)

Braithwaite, Rodric, *Afgantsy: The Russians in Afghanistan, 1979–89* (Profile Books, 2011)

Brigot, André, and Roy, Olivier, *The War in Afghanistan* (Harvester Wheatsheaf, 1988)

Collins, Joseph, *The Soviet Invasion of Afghanistan: A Study in the Use of Force* (D.C. Heath Canada, 1986)

Collins, Kathleen, *The Logic of Clan Politics in Central Asia* (CUP, 2006)

Cordesman, Anthony and Wagner, Abraham, *The Lessons of Modern War. Vol. III: The Afghan and Falklands Conflicts* (Westview Press, 1990)

Cordovez, Diego and Harrison, Selig, *Out of Afghanistan: The Inside Story of the Soviet Withdrawal* (OUP, 1995)

Crile, George, *Charlie Wilson's War: The Extraordinary Account of the Largest Covert Operation in History* (Atlantic Monthly Press, 2003)

Dupree, Louis, *Afghanistan* (OUP, 1997)

Emadi, Hafizullah, *Culture and Customs of Afghanistan* (Greenwood, 2005)

Ewans, Martin, *Afghanistan: A Short History of Its People and Politics* (HarperCollins, 2002)

Feifer, G., *The Great Gamble: The Soviet War in Afghanistan* (HarperCollins, 2009)

Fremont-Barnes, Gregory, *The Anglo-Afghan Wars 1839–1919* (Osprey, 2009)

Galeotti, Mark, *Afghanistan: The Soviet Union's Last War* (Routledge, 2001)

Gall, Sandy, *Afghanistan: Agony of a Nation* (Bodley Head, 1988)

Gall, Sandy, *Afghanistan: Travels with the Mujahedeen* (New English Library, 1989)

Gandomi, J., *Lessons from the Soviet Occupation in Afghanistan for the United States and NATO* (Princeton UP, 2008)

Girardet, Edward, *Afghanistan: The Soviet War* (New York, NY: St. Martin's Press, 1985)

Giustozzi, Antonio, *War, Politics and Society in Afghanistan, 1978–1992* (Hurst & Co., 2000)

Goodson, Larry, *Afghanistan's Endless War: State Failure, Regional Politics, and the Rise of the Taliban* (University of Washington Press, 2001)

Grasselli, Gabriella, *British and American Responses to the Soviet Invasion of Afghanistan* (Dartmouth Publishing, 1996)

Grau, Lester, *The Bear Went Over the Mountain: Soviet Combat Tactics in Afghanistan* (Routledge, 1988)

Grau, Lester, and Gress, Michael, *The Soviet–Afghan War: How a Superpower*

Fought and Lost (University Press of Kansas, 2002)

Hammond, T., *Red Flag over Afghanistan: The Communist Coup, the Soviet Invasion and the Consequences* (Westview Press, 1984)

Hyman, Anthony, *Afghanistan under Soviet Domination, 1964–91* (Macmillan, 1992)

Isby, David, *Russia's War in Afghanistan* (Osprey, 1986)

Isby, David, *War in a Distant Country: Afghanistan – Invasion and Resistance* (Arms and Armour Press, 1989)

Jalali, Ali Ahmad, and Grau, Lester, *The Other Side of the Mountain: Mujahideen Tactics in the Soviet–Afghan War* (Military Press, 2001)

Jalali, Ali Ahmad, and Grau, Lester, *Afghan Guerrilla Warfare: In the Words of the Mujahideen Fighters* (Compendium Publishing, 2001)

Johnson, Rob, *The Afghan Way of War – Culture and Pragmatism: A Critical History* (Hurst & Co., 2011)

Jones, Ellen, *Red Army and Society: A Sociology of the Soviet Military* (Allen & Unwin, 1985)

Kakar, Hasan, *Afghanistan: The Soviet Invasion and the Afghan Response, 1979–82* (University of California Press, 1997)

Kaplan, Robert, *Soldiers of God: With Islamic Warriors in Afghanistan and Pakistan* (Vintage Books, 2001)

Keller, Shoshana, *To Moscow, Not Mecca: The Soviet Campaign against Islam in Central Asia* (Praeger Publishing, 2001)

Khan, Riaz, *Untying the Knot: Negotiating Soviet Withdrawal* (Duke UP, 1991)

Loyn, David, *Butcher and Bolt* (Windmill Books, 2009)

McMichael, Scott, *Stumbling Bear: Soviet Military Performance in Afghanistan* (Brassey's, 1991)

Magnus, Ralph, and Naby, Eden, *Afghanistan: Mullah, Marx and Mujahid* (West View Press, 1998)

Maley, William, *The Afghanistan Wars* (Palgrave Macmillan, 2009)

Mendelson, Sarah, *Changing Course: Ideas, Politics, and the Soviet Withdrawal from Afghanistan* (Princeton UP, 1998)

Ministry of Defence, United Kingdom, *Army Field Manual. Vol. 1, Part 10: Countering Insurgency* (MoD, 2010)

Nojumi, Neamatollah, *The Rise of the Taliban in Afghanistan* (Palgrave Macmillan, 2002)

Odom, W., *The Collapse of the Soviet Military* (Yale UP, 1998)

Prado, J., *Safe for Democracy: The Secret Wars of the CIA* (Ivar R. Dee, 2006)

Rasanaygam, Angelo, *Afghanistan: A Modern History* (I.B. Tauris, 2005)

Roy, Olivier, *Islam and Resistance in Afghanistan* (CUP, 1986)

Roy, Olivier, *The Lessons of the Soviet–Afghan War* (Nuffield Press, 1991)

Rubin, Barnett, *The Fragmentation of Afghanistan* (Yale UP, 1995)

Russian General Staff, ed. Lester Grau and Michael Gress, *The Soviet–Afghan War: How a Superpower Fought and Lost* (University Press of Kansas, 2002)

Saikal, Amin, *Modern Afghanistan: A History of Struggle and Survival* (I.B. Tauris, 2004)

Saikal, Amin, and Maley, William, *The Soviet Withdrawal from Afghanistan* (CUP, 1989)

Sarin, Oleg, and Dvoretsky, Lev, *The Afghan Syndrome: The Soviet Union's Vietnam* (Presidio Press, 1993)

Schofield, Carey, *The Russian Elite: Inside Spetsnaz and the Airborne Forces* (Greenhill Books, 1993)

Tamarov, Vladislav, *Afghanistan: A Russian Soldier's Story* (Ten Speed Press, 2005)

Tanner, S., *Afghanistan: A Military History from Alexander the Great to the War Against the Taliban* (Perseus Books Group, 2009)

Tomsen, Peter, *The Wars of Afghanistan: Messianic Terrorism, Tribal Conflicts, and the Failure of Great Powers* (Public Affairs, 2011)

Urban, Mark, *War in Afghanistan* (Macmillan, 1990)

Weinbaum, Martin, *Pakistan and Afghanistan: Resistance and Reconstruction* (Westview Press, 1994)

Yousaf, Mohammad, and Adkin, Mark, *The Battle for Afghanistan: The Soviets Versus the Mujahideen during the 1980s* (Pen & Sword, 2007)

Index

References to illustrations are shown in **bold**.